ISBN 0-8373-6747-6

CS-47   GENERAL APTITUDE AND ABILITIES SERIES

This is your
PASSBOOK® for...

Logical Reasoning

Test Preparation Study Guide

Questions & Answers

NLC

NATIONAL LEARNING CORPORATION

Copyright © 2016 by

National Learning Corporation

212 Michael Drive, Syosset, New York 11791

(516) 921-8888
(800) 645-6337
FAX: (516) 921-8743
www.passbooks.com
sales @ passbooks.com
info @ passbooks.com

PRINTED IN THE UNITED STATES OF AMERICA

PASSBOOK®

NOTICE

This book is SOLELY intended for, is sold ONLY to, and its use is RESTRICTED to *individual*, bona fide applicants or candidates who qualify by virtue of having seriously filed applications for appropriate license, certificate, professional and/or promotional advancement, higher school matriculation, scholarship, or other legitimate requirements of educational and/or governmental authorities.

This book is NOT intended for use, class instruction, tutoring, training, duplication, copying, reprinting, excerption, or adaptation, etc., by:

(1) Other publishers

(2) Proprietors and/or Instructors of "Coaching" and/or Preparatory Courses

(3) Personnel and/or Training Divisions of commercial, industrial, and governmental organizations

(4) Schools, colleges, or universities and/or their departments and staffs, including teachers and other personnel

(5) Testing Agencies or Bureaus

(6) Study groups which seek by the purchase of a single volume to copy and/or duplicate and/or adapt this material for use by the group as a whole without having purchased individual volumes for each of the members of the group

(7) Et al.

Such persons would be in violation of appropriate Federal and State statutes.

PROVISION OF LICENSING AGREEMENTS. — Recognized educational commercial, industrial, and governmental institutions and organizations, and others legitimately engaged in educational pursuits, including training, testing, and measurement activities, may address a request for a licensing agreement to the copyright owners, who will determine whether, and under what conditions, including fees and charges, the materials in this book may be used by them. In other words, a licensing facility exists for the legitimate use of the material in this book on other than an individual basis. However, it is asseverated and affirmed here that the material in this book *CANNOT* be used without the receipt of the express permission of such a licensing agreement from the Publishers.

NATIONAL LEARNING CORPORATION
212 Michael Drive
Syosset, New York 11791

Inquiries re licensing agreements should be addressed to:
The President
National Learning Corporation
212 Michael Drive
Syosset, New York 11791

PASSBOOK® SERIES

THE *PASSBOOK® SERIES* has been created to prepare applicants and candidates for the ultimate academic battlefield — the examination room.

At some time in our lives, each and every one of us may be required to take an examination — for validation, matriculation, admission, qualification, registration, certification, or licensure.

Based on the assumption that every applicant or candidate has met the basic formal educational standards, has taken the required number of courses, and read the necessary texts, the *PASSBOOK® SERIES* furnishes the one special preparation which may assure passing with confidence, instead of failing with insecurity. Examination questions — together with answers — are furnished as the basic vehicle for study so that the mysteries of the examination and its compounding difficulties may be eliminated or diminished by a sure method.

This book is meant to help you pass your examination provided that you qualify and are serious in your objective.

The entire field is reviewed through the huge store of content information which is succinctly presented through a provocative and challenging approach — the question-and-answer method.

A climate of success is established by furnishing the correct answers at the end of each test.

You soon learn to recognize types of questions, forms of questions, and patterns of questioning. You may even begin to anticipate expected outcomes.

You perceive that many questions are repeated or adapted so that you can gain acute insights, which may enable you to score many sure points.

You learn how to confront new questions, or types of questions, and to attack them confidently and work out the correct answers.

You note objectives and emphases, and recognize pitfalls and dangers, so that you may make positive educational adjustments.

Moreover, you are kept fully informed in relation to new concepts, methods, practices, and directions in the field.

You discover that you are actually taking the examination all the time: you are preparing for the examination by "taking" an examination, not by reading extraneous and/or supererogatory textbooks.

In short, this PASSBOOK®, used directedly, should be an important factor in helping you to pass your test.

LOGICAL REASONING

Logical reasoning questions test the ability to understand, analyze, and evaluate arguments. Some of the abilities tested by specific questions include recognizing the point of an argument, recognizing assumptions on which an argument is based, drawing conclusions from given premises, inferring material missing from given passages, applying principles governing one argument to another, identifying methods of argument, evaluating arguments and counterarguments, and analyzing evidence.

Each question or group of questions is based on a short argument, generally an excerpt from the kind of material graduate students are likely to encounter in their academic and personal reading. Although arguments may be drawn from specific fields of study such as philosophy, literary criticism, social studies, and the physical sciences, materials from more familiar sources such as political speeches, advertisements, and informal discussions or dialogues also form the basis for some questions. No specialized knowledge of any particular field is required for answering the questions, however, and no knowledge of the terminology of formal logic is presupposed.

Specific questions asked about the arguments draw on information obtained by the process of critical and analytical reading described above.

The following strategies may be helpful in answering logical reasoning questions:

The passage on which a question (or questions) is based should be read very carefully with close attention to such matters as (1) what is said specifically about a subject, (2) what is not said but necessarily follows from what is said, (3) what is suggested or claimed without substantiation in what is said. In addition, the means of relating statements, inferences, and claims - the structure of the argument- should be noted. Such careful reading may lead to the conclusion that the argument presented proceeds in an unsound or illogical fashion, but in many cases there will be no apparent weakness in the argument. It is important, in reading the arguments given, to attend to the soundness of the method employed and not to the actual truth of opinions presented.

It is important to determine exactly what information the questtion is asking for; for instance, although it might be expected that one would be asked to detect or name the most glaring fault in a weak argument, the question posed may actually ask for the selection of one of a group of other arguments that reveals the same fault. In some cases, questions may ask for a negative response, for instance, a weakness that is NOT found in an argument or a conclusion that CANNOT be drawn from an argument.

LOGICAL REASONING

DIRECTIONS: The questions in this section require you to follow or evaluate the reasoning contained in brief statements or passages. In some questions, each of the choices is a conceivable solution to the particular problem posed. However, you are to select the one that answers the question *best,* that is, the one that does not require you to make what are, by common-sense standards, implausible, superfluous, or incompatible assumptions. After you have chosen the best answer, print the letter of the correct answer in the space at the right.

Questions 1-2.

Despite their progress in civilization, men have not yet outgrown the chicken coop. Man, too, has his "pecking order," and those who have been victims will require victims.

1.   The paragraph would be *most appropriately* used in an argument   1.____

   A.   for industrial progress
   B.   against the evils that result from progress
   C.   against rigid class sytems
   D.   for humane treatment of animals
   E.   for more effective military tactics

2.   Which of the following assumptions underlie(s) the paragraph?   2.____
      I.   Men cannot avoid behaving as their animal ancestors did.
      II.   Progress in civilization is possible.
      III.   Those who are victimized by one fear all.
   The *CORRECT* answer is:

   A.   I only   B.   II only   C.   III only
   D.   I and III   E.   I, II, and III

3.   All ice creams are delicious.   3.____
   No delicious dishes are wholesome.
   This dish is sauerkraut.
   Given the premises above, which of the following could *NOT* be true?
      I.   The sauerkraut is both wholesome and delicious.
      II.   The sauerkraut is either wholesome or delicious.
      III.   The sauerkraut is neither wholesome nor delicious.
   The *CORRECT* answer is:

   A.   I only   B.   II only   C.   III only
   D.   I and II   E.   I and III

4.   All members of the advisory committee, appointed by each mayor to serve during his   4.____
   term, must belong to registered political parties.
   The only registered political parties in town are the Progressive and Monarchist parties.
   The present mayor is a Monarchist noted for his strong party bias.
   On the basis of the evidence stated above, which of the following conclusions is *most likely* to be TRUE?

A. The present mayor has been a Monarchist all of his life.
B. All members of the advisory committee have usually belonged to the party to which the mayor belonged.
C. The present mayor's advisory committee has some Monarchists appointed to serve only during his term.
D. Everyone in town professes loyalty to either the Progressive or the Monarchist party.
E. The Progressive and Monarchist parties recommend to the mayor candidates for the advisory committee.

———

KEY (CORRECT ANSWERS)

1. C
2. B
3. A
4. C

———

HOW TO TAKE A TEST

You have studied long, hard and conscientiously.

With your official admission card in hand, and your heart pounding, you have been admitted to the examination room.

You note that there are several hundred other applicants in the examination room waiting to take the same test.

They all appear to be equally well prepared.

You know that nothing but your best effort will suffice. The "moment of truth" is at hand: you now have to demonstrate objectively, in writing, your knowledge of content and your understanding of subject matter.

You are fighting the most important battle of your life—to pass and/or score high on an examination which will determine your career and provide the economic basis for your livelihood.

What extra, special things should you know and should you do in taking the examination?

BEFORE THE TEST

YOUR PHYSICAL CONDITION IS IMPORTANT

     If you are not well, you can't do your best work on tests. If you are half asleep, you can't do your best either. Here are some tips:

1) Get about the same amount of sleep you usually get. Don't stay up all night before the test, either partying or worrying—DON'T DO IT!
2) If you wear glasses, be sure to wear them when you go to take the test. This goes for hearing aids, too.
3) If you have any physical problems that may keep you from doing your best, be sure to tell the person giving the test. If you are sick or in poor health, you really cannot do your best on any test. You can always come back and take the test some other time.

AT THE TEST

EXAMINATION TECHNIQUES

1) Read the general instructions carefully. These are usually printed on the first page of the exam booklet. As a rule, these instructions refer to the timing of the examination; the fact that you should not start work until the signal and must stop work at a signal, etc. If there are any *special* instructions, such as a choice of questions to be answered, make sure that you note this instruction carefully.

2) When you are ready to start work on the examination, that is as soon as the signal has been given, read the instructions to each question booklet, underline any key words or phrases, such as *least, best, outline, describe* and the like. In this way you will tend to answer as requested rather than discover on reviewing your paper that you *listed without describing*, that you selected the *worst* choice rather than the *best* choice, etc.

3) If the examination is of the objective or multiple-choice type – that is, each question will also give a series of possible answers: A, B, C or D, and you are called upon to select the best answer and write the letter next to that answer on your answer paper – it is advisable to start answering each question in turn. There may be anywhere from 50 to 100 such questions in the three or four hours allotted and you can see how much time would be taken if you read through all the questions before beginning to answer any. Furthermore, if you come across a question or group of questions which you know would be difficult to answer, it would undoubtedly affect your handling of all the other questions.

4) If the examination is of the essay type and contains but a few questions, it is a moot point as to whether you should read all the questions before starting to answer any one. Of course, if you are given a choice – say five out of seven and the like – then it is essential to read all the questions so you can eliminate the two which are most difficult. If, however, you are asked to answer all the questions, there may be danger in trying to answer the easiest one first because you may find that you will spend too much time on it. The best technique is to answer the first question, then proceed to the second, etc.

5) Time your answers. Before the exam begins, write down the time it started, then add the time allowed for the examination and write down the time it must be completed, then divide the time available somewhat as follows:
   - If 3-1/2 hours are allowed, that would be 210 minutes. If you have 80 objective-type questions, that would be an average of 2-1/2 minutes per question. Allow yourself no more than 2 minutes per question, or a total of 160 minutes, which will permit about 50 minutes to review.
   - If for the time allotment of 210 minutes there are 7 essay questions to answer, that would average about 30 minutes a question. Give yourself only 25 minutes per question so that you have about 35 minutes to review.

6) The most important instruction is to *read each question* and make sure you know what is wanted. The second most important instruction is to *time yourself properly* so that you answer every question. The third most important instruction is to *answer every question*. Guess if you have to but include something for each question. Remember that you will receive no credit for a blank and will probably receive some credit if you write something in answer to an essay question. If you guess a letter – say "B" for a multiple-choice question – you may have guessed right. If you leave a blank as an answer to a multiple-choice question, the examiners may respect your

feelings but it will not add a point to your score. Some exams may penalize you for wrong answers, so in such cases *only*, you may not want to guess unless you have some basis for your answer.

7) Suggestions
   a. Objective-type questions
      1. Examine the question booklet for proper sequence of pages and questions
      2. Read all instructions carefully
      3. Skip any question which seems too difficult; return to it after all other questions have been answered
      4. Apportion your time properly; do not spend too much time on any single question or group of questions
      5. Note and underline key words – *all, most, fewest, least, best, worst, same, opposite,* etc.
      6. Pay particular attention to negatives
      7. Note unusual option, e.g., unduly long, short, complex, different or similar in content to the body of the question
      8. Observe the use of "hedging" words – *probably, may, most likely,* etc.
      9. Make sure that your answer is put next to the same number as the question
      10. Do not second-guess unless you have good reason to believe the second answer is definitely more correct
      11. Cross out original answer if you decide another answer is more accurate; do not erase until you are ready to hand your paper in
      12. Answer all questions; guess unless instructed otherwise
      13. Leave time for review

   b. Essay questions
      1. Read each question carefully
      2. Determine exactly what is wanted. Underline key words or phrases.
      3. Decide on outline or paragraph answer
      4. Include many different points and elements unless asked to develop any one or two points or elements
      5. Show impartiality by giving pros and cons unless directed to select one side only
      6. Make and write down any assumptions you find necessary to answer the questions
      7. Watch your English, grammar, punctuation and choice of words
      8. Time your answers; don't crowd material

8) Answering the essay question

Most essay questions can be answered by framing the specific response around several key words or ideas. Here are a few such key words or ideas:

M's: manpower, materials, methods, money, management
P's: purpose, program, policy, plan, procedure, practice, problems, pitfalls, personnel, public relations

a. Six basic steps in handling problems:
   1. Preliminary plan and background development
   2. Collect information, data and facts
   3. Analyze and interpret information, data and facts
   4. Analyze and develop solutions as well as make recommendations
   5. Prepare report and sell recommendations
   6. Install recommendations and follow up effectiveness

b. Pitfalls to avoid
   1. *Taking things for granted* – A statement of the situation does not necessarily imply that each of the elements is necessarily true; for example, a complaint may be invalid and biased so that all that can be taken for granted is that a complaint has been registered
   2. *Considering only one side of a situation* – Wherever possible, indicate several alternatives and then point out the reasons you selected the best one
   3. *Failing to indicate follow up* – Whenever your answer indicates action on your part, make certain that you will take proper follow-up action to see how successful your recommendations, procedures or actions turn out to be
   4. *Taking too long in answering any single question* – Remember to time your answers properly

EXAMINATION SECTION

EXAMINATION SECTION
TEST 1

DIRECTIONS: Each question or incomplete statement is followed by several suggested answers or completions. Select the one that BEST answers the question or completes the statement. *PRINT THE LETTER OF THE CORRECT ANSWER IN THE SPACE AT THE RIGHT.*

QUESTIONS 1-4.

Questions 1-4 refer to the following information.

A recent study shows that of the 1000 graduates of Learnmore High School, 40% claimed that they smoked during their high school years, 30% said they started smoking before entering high school and continued smoking during high school years. Of the people who didn't smoke at all during their high school year, 70% claim that they have no medical problems. However, only 10% of those who did smoke during their high school years reported no medical problem.

1. What percent of all these graduates claim they have NO medical problem?   1.____

    A. 30   B. 42
    C. 60   D. 70
    E. None of the above

2. How many non-smokers have had at LEAST one medical problem?   2.____

    A. 70   B. 180   C. 280   D. 350   E. 450

3. What is the MAXIMUM number of people who began smoking before entering high school, and have had NO medical problems?   3.____

    A. 10   B. 30   C. 40   D. 100   E. over 100

4. Counting only individuals who have experienced at least one medical problem, what is the ratio of those who didn't smoke during high school years to those who did smoke during that time period?   4.____

    A. 3:2   B. 1:2   C. 1:3   D. 2:3   E. 3:1

5. If John enjoys the taste of pineapple, he'll like the taste of all fruit. The preceding statement is MOST similar to which of the following?   5.____

    A. If a dog has a liking for human food, he'll like all dog food
    B. If a person can understand algebra, he can understand all mathematics
    C. If a Chevrolet gets good gas mileage, then so will a Datsun
    D. If Sue's favorite color is red, then she won't buy a green dress
    E. If Bob can fix any electrical item, then he can fix a toaster

6. Only a few people who are heavy smokers will live past the age of 90. Since Eve is a 30-year-old non-smoker, she will probably live beyond the age of 90.
The argument is MOST similar to which of the following?   6.____

A. Only a few cities like Cleanville have a low crime rate. Thus, if a person lives in a low crime rate city, that city must be Cleanville.
B. Only birds have feathers. Thus, some birds have morefeathers than other birds.
C. All weight-lifters are light sleepers. Since Bob is a heavy sleeper, he doesn't lift weights.
D. Not many individuals who worry a lot can get a good night's rest. Since John does not worry at all, he can probably get a good night's rest.
E. Some mathematicians enjoy all sports. Since William is a mathematician, he may not enjoy any sports.

7. Since Jack is left-handed, he is an excellent tennis player. Assuming that the preceding statement is true, from which one(s) of the following can this quoted statement be logically deduced?   7.____

    I.   All tennis players are left-handed.
    II. None of the excellent tennis players is right-handed.
    III. Either Jack is right-handed or he is an excellent tennis player.

A. I only   B. II only   C. III only
D. II and III   E. I, II, and III

8. Gamblers are boisterous individuals. Yesterday, I went to the racetrack and there was a lot of shouting after every race. The above argument assumes: 8.____

    I.   Gamblers frequent racetracks.
    II. Noisy people are gamblers.
    III. Quiet people don't go to racetracks.

A. I only   B. II only   C. III only
D. I, III   E. I, II, III

QUESTIONS 9-14.

Questions 9-14 refer to the facts below. It is to be assumed that it is the month of July, the first day of which is a Monday.

The Ail-Weather appliance store sells televisions, radios, toasters, and refrigerators. Certain conditions govern this store:

    I.   The store is open only Monday through Friday every month. Thus, all purchases and deliveries can only be made Monday through Friday.
    II. TV's and radios are only delivered on even numbered days.
    III. Refrigerators are delivered only on Tuesdays and Thursdays.
    IV. Toasters are delivered on any date of the month which can be divided evenly by 3 or 5.
    V. A customer may purchase a radio or a toaster on the day of delivery.
    VI. Since refrigerators and TV's are more expensive items, they are immediately inspected on the day of delivery. However, a customer may not purchase these items until 3 business days after delivery.

9. Which item(s) could be neither delivered nor purchased on Wednesdays?   9.____

A. TV's and radios   B. TV's, radios, and refrigerators
C. Refrigerators and toasters   D. Refrigerators *only*
E. Toasters *only*

10. On how many days during this month can toasters be purchased?   10.____

    A. At least 4 but fewer than 7   B. 9
    C. 11   D. More than 11
    E. None of the above

11. During the first week, on which dates may a TV either be purchased or delivered?   11.____

    A. 2nd, 3rd, 4th   B. 2nd, 4th, 5th   C. 3rd, 4th, 5th
    D. 2nd, 5th, 6th   E. 2nd, 3rd

12. On how many days during this month can TV's be delivered?   12.____

    A. Fewer than 6   B. 8   C. 9
    D. 10   E. 11

13. What is the *earliest* date on which both a TV and toaster can be purchased?   13.____

    A. 3rd   B. 5th   C. 7th   D. 9th   E. 11th

14. Which appliance(s) has(have) exactly 2 delivery dates on Fridays?   14.____

    A. Toasters, radios, TV's   B. Toasters, TV's
    C. TV's, radios   D. Toasters, radios
    E. Only toasters

15. If a person studies hard, he can pass any high school course.   15.____
    This statement can be logically deduced from which of the following?

    A. Some people study while others don't study.
    B. A person who has passed a particular high school course must have studied hard.
    C. A high school course can be passed if a person is willing to study hard.
    D. If a person doesn't study, he can't expect to pass a high school course.
    E. Some high school courses require more studying than do other courses.

QUESTIONS 16-17.

Questions 16 and 17 are to be answered on the basis of the following.

    The most dangerous sport in the world is thoroughbred horseracing, since more partici-
pants per thousand are killed than in any other sport. Hang-gliding is the second most
dangerous sport. By contrast, boxing ranks tenth on the list of most dangerous sports.

16. The author of the above paragraph is *most likely* trying to convey the message that: 16.____

    A. Most sports are dangerous
    B. Hang-gliding is popular despite its danger
    C. Only ten sports are considered dangerous
    D. The most number of injuries occur in horseracing
    E. Boxing is not the most dangerous sport

17. The author would *probably* be opposed to: 17.____

    A. Any dangerous sport
    B. A ban on boxing
    C. Amateur boxing
    D. Horseracing
    E. A ban on horseracing

QUESTIONS 18-22.

Questions 18-22 are to be answered on the basis of the following.
The Expanding Food Company has outlet stores on each of First Ave., Second Ave., Third Ave., Fourth Ave., and Fifth Ave. Also, it is known that:

    I. There is at least one store on each avenue.
    II. The number of stores on Fifth Ave. equals the sum of the number of stores on First Ave. plus those on Second Ave.
    III. The number of stores on Second Ave. is double the number of stores on Third Ave.
    IV. The number of stores on Fourth Ave. is greater than the number of stores on Fifth Ave.
    V. There are an even number of stores on First Ave.

18. What is the *fewest* number of stores that must exist on Fourth Ave.?   18.____

    A. 2   B. 3   C. 4   D. 5   E. 6

19. Which avenue has the MOST stores?   19.____

    A. Fifth Ave.   B. Fourth Ave.
    C. Third Ave.   D. All of the above
    E. None of the above

20. Suppose NO avenue has *more* than 7 stores. Find the total number of stores on all 5 avenues.   20.____

    A. 16 or 19   B. 20
    C. 21   D. 16, 19 or 20
    E. 16, 20 or 21

21. The number of stores on Fifth Ave   21.____

    A. must be even
    B. must be odd
    C. could equal the number of stores on First Ave.
    D. could equal the number of stores on Second Ave.
    E. none of the above

22. Suppose it is known that there are 4 stores on Third Ave. and that there are *more* than 4 stores on First Ave.   22.____
Find the *minimum* number of stores on all 5 avenues.

    A. 45   B. 49   C. 46   D. 48   E. 47

QUESTIONS 23-25.

Questions 23 through 25 are to be answered on the basis of the following.

In a particular group of 21 people, each individual is one of three professions: doctor, engineer, or teacher. Half the number of people who smoke are engineers. One-third of the number of non-smokers are doctors. The number of engineers who smoke equals the number of non-smokers who are not doctors.

23. How many of the non-smokers are doctors?   23._____

    A. 2   B. 3   C. 5   D. 6   E. 9

24. If all the teachers are smokers, and there are only 2 doctors who smoke, then the teachers represent _____ Percent of the entire group.   24._____

    A. 19   B. 25   C. 29   D. 33   E. 40

25. Using the information from the preceding question, *how many* engineers are there in the entire group?   25._____

    A. 3   B. 6   C. 9   D. 12   E. 15

KEY (CORRECT ANSWERS)

1.	E		11.	B
2.	B		12.	E
3.	C		13.	B
4.	B		14.	A
5.	B		15.	C
6.	D		16.	E
7.	C		17.	B
8.	A		18.	D
9.	D		19.	B
10.	E		20.	E

21.	A
22.	E
23.	B
24.	A
25.	D

SOLUTIONS

1. (.70)(.60) = .42 of all the graduates didn't smoke and didn't have any medical problems, whereas (.10)(.40) = .04 of all the graduates did smoke but yet didn't experience any medical problems. Thus, .42 + .04 = .46 or 46% of all graduates claimed they had no medical problems.

    (ANSWER E).

2. (.30)(.60) = .18 of the population were non-smokers and yet had at least one medical problem. Now (.18)(1000) = 180.

    (ANSWER B).

3. (.10)(.40) = .04 indicates the number of people who did smoke during their high school years and had no medical problem. Of the .04, it is not possible to determine what fraction actually started smoking before entering high school. So, (.04)(1000) = 40.

    (ANSWER C).

4. (.30)(.60) = .18 of the non-smokers had at least one medical problem, whereas (.90)(.40) = .36 of the smokers had at least one medical problem. Then .18/.36 = 1:2 ratio.

    (ANSWER B).

5. The original statement uses the truth of a specific item in order to imply the truth of a general item containing that specific item. Only choice B illustrates that kind of reasoning.

    (ANSWER B).

6. The original statement can be written: "If A, then B. If not A, then not B." This argument is not necessarily valid, but choice D resembles it most closely.

    (ANSWER D).

7. Statement I is false, since we can assume that there exist both left-handed and right-handed players. Statement II is also false, because there may be excellent right-handed players. Statement III is true, since Jack is not right-handed and thus would have to be an excellent tennis player.

    (ANSWER C).

8. The only valid implication is Statement I, since one can assume that gamblers do visit racetracks. (This statement could be false, since it is only an assumption). Statement II is not valid since many types of people are noisy. Statement III is also invalid since one can assume that both noisy and quiet people frequent racetracks.

    (ANSWER A).

QUESTIONS 9-14.

Questions 9-14 see calendars below showing days of receiving and purchasing of each of the 4 different appliances. Note that for question #10, the actual answer is 10.

Radio Delivered / TV Delivered

Sun	Mon	Tu	Wed	Th	Fri	Sat
	1	(2)	3	(4)	5	6
7	(8)	9	(10)	11	(12)	13
14	15	(16)	17	(18)	19	20
21	(22)	23	(24)	25	(26)	27
28	29	(30)	31			

Toaster Delivered

Sun	Mon	Tu	Wed	Th	Fri	Sat
	1	2	(3)	4	(5)	6
7	8	(9)	(10)	11	(12)	13
14	(15)	16	17	(18)	19	20
21	22	23	(24)	(25)	26	27
28	29	(30)	31			

Refrigerator Delivered

Sun	Mon	Tu	Wed	Th	Fri	Sat
	1	(2)	3	(4)	5	6
7	8	(9)	10	(11)	12	13
14	15	(16)	17	(18)	19	20
21	22	(23)	24	(25)	26	27
28	29	(30)	31			

Radio Purchased

Sun	Mon	Tu	Wed	Th	Fri	Sat
	1	(2)	3	(4)	5	6
7	(8)	9	(10)	11	(12)	13
14	15	(16)	17	(18)	19	20
21	(22)	23	(24)	25	(26)	27
28	29	(30)	31			

Radio Purchased

Sun	Mon	Tu	Wed	Th	Fri	Sat
	1	(2)	3	(4)	5	6
7	(8)	9	(10)	11	(12)	13
14	15	(16)	17	(18)	19	20
21	(22)	23	(24)	25	(26)	27
28	29	(30)	31			

Toaster Purchased

Sun	Mon	Tu	Wed	Th	Fri	Sat
	1	2	(3)	4	(5)	6
7	8	(9)	(10)	11	(12)	13
14	(15)	16	17	(18)	19	20
21	22	23	(24)	(25)	26	27
28	29	(30)	31			

TV Purchased

Sun	Mon	Tu	Wed	Th	Fri	Sat
	1	2	3	4	(5)	6
7	8	(9)	10	(11)	12	13
14	(15)	16	(17)	18		20
21	22	(23)	24	(25)	26	27
28	(29)	30	(31)			

Refrigerator Purchased

Sun	Mon	Tu	Wed	Th	Fri	Sat
	1	2	3	4	(5)	6
7	8	(9)	10	11	(12)	13
14	15	(16)	17	18	(19)	20
21	22	(23)	24	25	(26)	27
28	29	(30)	31			

9. (ANSWER D).

10. (ANSWER E).

11. (ANSWER B).

12. (ANSWER E).

13. (ANSWER B).

14. (ANSWER A).

15. The original statement follows logically from choice C, since it implies that studying hard is a prerequisite to passing any high school course.

(ANSWER C).

16. Although the general public perceives boxing as the most dangerous sport(or at least one of the most dangerous), the author is relying on a certain type of statistic to illustrate that there are nine other sports which could be considered more dangerous than boxing.

(ANSWER E).

17. The author, by his argument, appears to be defending any ban on the sport of boxing. He does not make any case for or against another sport.

(ANSWER B).

18. Let x, $2y$, y, w, z be the number of stores respectively on First, Second, Third, Fourth, and Fifth Avenues. Also, $z = x + 2y$, $w > z$, and x must be an even number. Since the smallest values for x and y are 2 and 1 respectively, the minimum value of $z = 2 + (2)(1) = 4$. Now $w =$ the number of stores on Fourth Ave., and since $w > z$, then $w > 4$. Thus, 5 is the minimum value of w.

(ANSWER D).

19. Since $z = x + 2y$, $z > x$ and $z > y$. But $w > z$, so that w is the variable with the highest value. We know that $w =$ the number of stores on Fourth Ave.

(ANSWER B).

20. Assume $z = 7$. Then there are two e possible combinations of numbers associated with the number of stores on First, Second, Third, Fourth, and Fifth Avenues respectively. The 1st combination is 2, 4, 2, 7, 6; the 2nd combination is 4, 2, 1, 7, 6; the 3rd combination is 2, 2, 1, 7, 4. Thus, only 16, 20, or 21 are the possible totals.

(ANSWER E).

21. Since $z = x + 2y$ and x must be even, then z must also be an even number. Note that $2y$ is already even. Thus, even number + even number = even number.

(ANSWER A).

22. Since Third Ave. has 4 stores, Second Ave. has 8 stores. We also know that First Ave. has more than 4 stores; thus it must have a minimum of 6 stores (even number). Fifth Ave. has $6 + 8 = 14$ stores at minimum, and $15 =$ the minimum stores on Fourth Ave. Thus, the number of stores on all 5 avenues (minimum) $= 6 + 8 + 4 + 14 + 15 = 47$.

(ANSWER E).

23. Let $x = $ # of smokers, so that $21 - x = $ # of non-smokers. Then $1/2x = $ # of smokers who are also engineers. This number must equal the number of non-smokers who are not doctors. We can infer that 2/3 of the non-smokers (i.e. $2/3 [21 - x]$) are not doctors. Thus, $1/2x = 2/3 (21 - x)$. So, $x = 12$ and $21 - x = 9$. This implies that there are a total of 9 non-smokers. Since 1/3 of this number are doctors, there are 3 non-smoking doctors.

(ANSWER B).

24. Since 1/2 of the smokers are engineers, this translates to (1/2)(12) = 6 people. Only 2 doctors smoke, so the number of teachers who smoke = 12 - 6 - 2 = 4. (All teachers are smokers). Now 4/21 = .1905 or approximately 19%.

(ANSWER A).

25. The non-smokers must consist of only doctors and engineers. Of the 9 non-smokers, 3 are doctors. Thus 6 non-smokers are engineers. We already know that there are 6 engineers who smoke, so that there are a total of 12 engineers.

(ANSWER D).

———

LOGICAL REASONING

EXAMINATION SECTION
TEST 1

DIRECTIONS: Each question or incomplete statement is followed by several suggested answers or completions. Select the one that BEST answers the question or completes the Statement. *PRINT THE LETTER OF THE CORRECT ANSWER IN THE SPACE AT THE RIGHT.*

QUESTIONS 1-3.

For questions 1-3 an initial argument is presented. Of the five given choices, select the one that MOST closely resembles the argument.

1. A stove is usually hot. One often reads about a child who burns his hands by touching a stove.

    A. The weather is probably cool. I see several people wearing jackets.
    B. A science course is often difficult. One usually hears a high school student complain about science exams.
    C. High school football is sometimes dangerous. Players often do not take proper precautions.
    D. A person can learn to appreciate art. However, not all people will become artists.
    E. Bowling alleys are normally crowded. Yet some people enjoy waiting several hours in order to bowl.

1._____

2. Joseph lives in New Jersey. Newark is located in New Jersey. Therefore, Joseph lives in Newark.

    A. The letter A is a vowel. Vowels are part of the alphabet. Therefore, the letter A is part of the alphabet.
    B. Susan enjoys bowling. John enjoys tennis. Therefore, Susan and John are not compatible.
    C. Bob goes to Central High School. Mathematics is taught at Central High School. Therefore, Bob is taking mathematics.
    D. Jane play field hockey. Field hockey is considered a dangerous sport. Therefore, Jane plays a dangerous sport.
    E. All mammals drink water. Tables do not drink water. Therefore, tables are not mammals.

2._____

3. Not all libraries have phone directories. If they did, there would be less room to stock books.

    A. Some baseball umpires are honest. If they were not, it would be impossible to have baseball games.
    B. Some chemicals are poisonous. All labels on bottles indicate whether the contents are poisonous.
    C. All flags have stripes. If they did not, they would not be considered flags.
    D. Some restaurants do not have booths. If they had booths, there would not be ample space for counter seats.
    E. No city is safe. If they were, there would be no more crime.

3._____

QUESTIONS 4-11.

Questions 4-11 pertain to the following.

A college student has four vertical shelves mounted in his dorm. Each shelf is assigned a subject title, corresponding to each of the four subjects he is taking. Those subjects are math, English, chemistry, and history. Also it is known that:

1. There is AT LEAST one book on each shelf.
2. The shelf for English books is two slots above the shelf for math books, but adjacent to the slot for chemistry books.
3. The shelf for chemistry books is NOT the top shelf.
4. The number of English books is three times the number of chemistry books.
5. The number of math books is five less than the number of English books, but more than the number of chemistry books.
6. The number of history books is more than the number of math books, but less than the number of English books.
7. The number of books on the third shelf does not exceed 20.

4. There are _____ chemistry books.　　　　　　　　　　　　　　　　　　　4.___

    A. at least 2
    B. at most 6
    C. between 3 and 5 inclusive
    D. between 3 and 6 inclusive
    E. either 4 or 5

5. The MINIMUM total number of books is　　　　　　　　　　　　　　　　5.___

    A. 20   B. 21   C. 22   D. 23   E. 24

6. Math books are found on the _____ shelf.　　　　　　　　　　　　　　6.___

    A. 1st or 2nd   B. 2nd or 3rd   C. 3rd
    D. 2nd   E. 1st

7. Which subject(s) will have NO books on neither the top nor bottom shelves?　　7.___

    A. math   B. English
    C. chemistry and English   D. chemistry
    E. math and history

8. The MAXIMUM number of books on the fourth shelf is　　　　　　　　　8.___

    A. 16   B. 18   C. 20
    D. 22   E. more than 22

9. Which pair of subject books CANNOT lie on adjacent shelves?　　　　　　9.___

    A. English and chemistry   B. chemistry and history
    C. history and English   D. history and math
    E. math and chemistry

10. In how many different ways can the subject titles be assigned to the four shelves?   10.____

    A. 1   B. 2   C. 3
    D. 4   E. at least 5

11. Which of the following could NOT be the number of history books?   11.____

    A. 15   B. 12   C. 9   D. 6   E. 3

QUESTIONS 12-16.

Questions 12-16 pertain to the following.

Lucky Charlie visited his favorite racetrack yesterday. There were a total of four races; in each race there were only six horses, numbers 1 through 6. The names of the winning horses were Lucky Molly, Mister Class, Super Power, and Great Lady. Also, it is known that:

 1. The number of the winning horse of each race was lower than the number of the winner of any previous race.
 2. The number 5 horse did not win the second race.
 3. An even numbered horse won the third race.
 4. Great Lady won the fourth race.
 5. Super Power's number is twice Lucky Molly's number.

12. What number did Great Lady have?   12.____

    A. 1   B. 2   C. 3 or 4   D. 5   E. 6

13. If Super Power won his race directly before Lucky Molly won her race, then Super Power's number is   13.____

    A. 1 or 2   B. 2 or 4   C. 4   D. 4 or 6   E. 6

14. How many different possibilities exist for the winning numbers for all four races?   14.____

    A. 1   B. 2   C. 3
    D. 4   E. at least 5

15. Mister Class won the _____ race and his number was _____.   15.____

    A. second, 2   B. third, 1   C. third, 4
    D. fourth, 4   E. first, 6

16. If the number 3 horse won the second race and Lucky Molly won the third race, then the CORRECT order of the winning horses in races 1, 2, 3, and 4 respectively is   16.____

    A. Super Power, Mister Class, Lucky Molly, Great Lady
    B. Mister Class, Great Lady, Lucky Molly, Super Power
    C. Great Lady, Super Power, Lucky Molly, Mister Class
    D. Mister Class, Super Power, Lucky Molly, Great Lady
    E. Super Power, Great Lady, Lucky Molly, Mister Class

QUESTIONS 17-19.

Questions 17-19 pertain to the following:

1. If A is true, then C is false.
2. If A is false, then B is true.
3. Either D is false or C is true.
4. It is possible that both D is false and C is true.

17. If B is true, then _____.   17.____

    A. A is false   B. D is true
    C. A is true   D. C is true
    E. no conclusion can be reached about A, C, or D

18. At least one of _____ or _____ is true.   18.____

    A. A, B   B. A, D
    C. B, opposite of C   D. D, opposite of C
    E. C, D

19. If D is true, then _____ is (are) true.   19.____

    A. C *only*   B. B *only*
    C. both A and B   D. both B and C
    E. both A and the opposite of B

QUESTIONS 20-25.

Questions 20-25 pertain to the following:

Alice has invented a word game in which each letter A through J is assigned one number from 1 through 10. It is possible, however, that two or more letters are assigned to the same number. In fact, the three vowels correspond to the same odd number. The letters B, D, and F correspond to three different even numbers. Each consonant, with one exception, has a higher numerical value than any vowel. Exactly one letter is worth 1. All consonants, except G, have an even numerical value. The value of C is higher than that of F, but lower than that of D. The value of J is 4 and no other letter has this value. The value of A is one half that of F. The value of H is higher than that of C.

20. How many letters have a value of 5?   20.____

    A. none   B. 1   C. 2
    D. 3   E. at least 4

21. B has the same value as   21.____

    A. C   B. D   C. E   D. G   E. H

22. Which letter has a value of 6?   22.____

    A. none   B. A   C. F   D. G   E. H

23. The value of I is   23.____

    A. 1   B. 3   C. 5   D. 7   E. 9

24. The value of J is _____ the value of D. 24.____

    A. 1/4   B. 1/2   C. 1/3
    D. 2/3   E. none of these

25. Which pair of letters has values which are consecutive numbers? 25.____

    A. A, C   B. F, G   C. D, H   D. B, D   E. I, J

KEY (CORRECT ANSWERS)

1.	B		11.	E
2.	C		12.	A
3.	D		13.	D
4.	D		14.	D
5.	B		15.	E
6.	A		16.	A
7.	D		17.	E
8.	B		18.	C
9.	B		19.	D
10.	B		20.	A

21.	A
22.	C
23.	B
24.	E
25.	E

SOLUTIONS TO PROBLEMS

1. The first sentence states a general conclusion, which is substantiated by information that an individual might have read or heard about. Only choice B presents that same type of logic pattern.

   (ANSWER B).

2. The logic presented here is faulty, since two facts may imply a third fact without implying each other. In choice C, the conclusion is structured as one of two statements implying the other simply because they are both related to a third statement.

   (ANSWER C).

3. A statement is given, followed by a justification in terms of "what-if". Note that the first statement takes the form of "not all," which can be interpreted as "some" or "at least one". Choice D is most closely structured in this way.

   (ANSWER D).

4. Let x = number of chemistry books. Then $3x$ = number of English books and $3x - 5$ = number of math books. It is also known that $3x$ > number of history books > $3x - 5$. It can be determined that the correct order of subjects from the first through fourth shelves is: history, math, chemistry, English, or math, chemistry, English, history. Thus $3x \leq 20$, so $x \leq 6$. Since the number of math books has to be at least 2, $3x - 5 \geq 2$, which means $x \geq 3$ (whole numbers only). Thus $3 \leq$ number of chemistry books ≤ 6.

   (ANSWER E).

5. Since 3 is the least number of chemistry books, the least number of English, math, and history books are 9, 4, and 5 respectively. The total is 21.

   (ANSWER B).

6. Refer to explanation for #4.

   (ANSWER A).

7. Refer to explanation for #4.

   (ANSWER D).

8. Since only English or history books may appear on the fourth shelf, and the number of English books would be greater, we find the maximum value for $3x$. Since $x \leq 6$, $3x \leq 18$.

   (ANSWER B).

9. Either chemistry and history books will lie on the third and first shelves (respectively) or on the second and fourth shelves (respectively).

   (ANSWER B).

10. Refer to explanation in #4.

    (ANSWER B).

11. In question 5, we established that the actual least number of math books is 4; thus, the number of history books must *exceed* 4.

(ANSWER E).

12. Only four possibilities exist for the numbers of the winning horses in races 1 through 4 respectively.
Possibility 1: 6, 4, 2, 1 Possibility 2: 6, 3, 2, 1
Possibility 3: 5, 4, 2, 1 Possibility 4: 4, 3, 2, 1
Since Great Lady won the fourth race, her number was 1.

(ANSWER A).

13. Since Super Power's number is twice Lucky Molly's number, only the first three possibilities listed in #12's explanation could exist. Thus Super Power's number could only be 4 or 6.

(ANSWER D).

14. Refer to explanation for #12.

(ANSWER D).

15. If possibility 1 is true then Mister Class had to win the first race and his number was 6. If possibility 2 is true, Mister Class had to win the third race and his number was 2. If possibility 3 is true, Mister Class had to win the first race and his number was 5. Finally, if possibility 4 is true, then Mister Class won the second race and his number was 3.

(ANSWER E).

16. Only possibility 4 would be correct, so that the winning numbers of the four races are 4, 3, 2, 1 respectively. Since Super Power's number is twice Lucky Molly's number, their numbers are 4 and 2 respectively. Great Lady's number is 1; thus Mister Class' number is 4.

(ANSWER A).

17. Since B and D cannot both be true, and B is true, then D must be false. By Statement 3, C can be true or false.

(ANSWER E).

18. Exactly one will happen: Either B being true or C being false. By Statement 2, if B were false, A would be true (contrapositive). Then, Statement 1 says that C is false.

(ANSWER C).

19. By Statement 3, if D is true, C must be true. Then, the contrapositive of statement 1 says that A is false. Furthermore, by Statement 2, B must be true.

(ANSWER D).

For questions 20-25, the following chart shows the allowable letter(s) for each number 1 through 10:

1 = G	6 = F
2 = none	7 = none
3 = A, E, I	8 = B, C
4 = J	9 = none
5 = none	10 = D, H

Note that all questions 20-25 can be answered based on the above chart. In #24 choice E is correct since the ratio of values of J and D is 4/10 or 2/5..

———

EXAMINATION SECTION
TEST 1

DIRECTIONS: Each question or incomplete statement is followed by several suggested answers or completions. Select the one that BEST answers the question or completes the statement. *PRINT THE LETTER OF THE CORRECT ANSWER IN THE SPACE AT THE RIGHT.*

Questions 1-7.

DIRECTIONS: Questions 1 through 7 are to be answered based on the following set of facts.

The four towns of Alpha, Beta, Gamma, and Delta lie in a straight line from left to right, but not necessarily in that order. Each town has a different maximum speed limit, and each maximum speed limit ends in 0 or 5. Delta lies to the east of Beta. Alpha lies east of Beta, but west of Delta. The distance between Beta and Alpha equals the distance between Alpha and Delta. Alpha and Gamma are adjacent towns. Gamma and Delta are 50 miles apart. The distance between Alpha and Gamma is less than 10 miles.

Concerning the maximum speed limits, Beta's is one-third that of Alpha's, Delta's is higher than Alpha's by 10 m.p.h., and Gamma has the highest. No town's maximum speed limit exceeds 80 m.p.h. nor is less than 20 m.p.h.

1. Which of the following is the CORRECT order of towns from west to east?   1.____

   A. Beta, Delta, Gamma, Alpha   B. Beta, Alpha, Gamma, Delta
   C. Delta, Alpha, Gamma, Beta   D. Gamma, Alpha, Beta, Delta
   E. Delta, Gamma, Alpha, Beta

2. What is Gamma's MAXIMUM speed limit in m.p.h.?   2.____

   A. 65   B. 70   C. Over 70
   D. 60   E. Under 60

3. What is the ratio of Beta's MAXIMUM speed limit to that of Delta?   3.____

   A. 4:15   B. 1:3   C. 1:4   D. 3:5   E. 2:7

4. Suppose that next year Beta's maximum speed limit is tripled, and Alpha's is reduced by 5 m.p.h.   4.____
   What would be the CORRECT order of towns from lowest to highest maximum speed limit?

   A. Delta, Alpha, Beta, Gamma   B. Beta, Delta, Alpha, Gamma
   C. Alpha, Delta, Beta, Gamma   D. Alpha, Beta, Delta, Gamma
   E. Beta, Alpha, Gamma, Delta

5. What is the distance, in miles, between Delta and Alpha?   5.____

   A. Between 50 and 55 inclusive   B. Under 50
   C. Over 55 but under 65   D. Over 50 but under 60
   E. Over 60

6. The distance between Beta and Delta must be less than _____ miles.   6.__

    A. 50   B. 65   C. 75   D. 90   E. 120

7. For which towns can the EXACT maximum speed limit be determined?   7.__

    A. Alpha and Gamma   B. Alpha, Beta, and Delta
    C. Beta, Delta, and Gamma   D. Beta and Gamma
    E. All four towns

Questions 8-14.

DIRECTIONS: Questions 8 through 14 are to be answered based upon the following set of facts.

Johnny Quicksale sells three types of books: biographical, novels, and statistical. Each type of book comes in three different versions: condensed, regular, and expanded. For each type of book, the order of cost from least expensive to most expensive is condensed, regular, and expanded. Each type has a different price, and the pricing between books is somewhat involved. Condensed statistical books cost more than both regular novels and regular biographies, but less than expanded novels. Expanded biographies cost less than regular novels, but more than condensed novels. Condensed biographies are the cheapest. Expanded statistical books are not the most expensive. The price for each condensed and regular book is a multiple of $5, whereas the price of each expanded book is a multiple of $25. Each book sells for less than $95. A regular statistical book costs less than $45.

8. The CORRECT sequence of the first three books (in increasing price) starting from the cheapest is: 8.__

    A. Condensed biography, regular biography, consensed novel
    B. Condensed novel, condensed biography, condensed statistical
    C. Condensed statistical, condensed novel, condensed biography
    D. Condensed novel, condensed biography, regular novel
    E. Condensed biography, condensed novel, regular biography

9. How many books cost over $10?   9.__

    A. 3   B. 4 or 5   C. 6   D. 7 or 8   E. all 9

10. If just the expanded versions were listed in correct order from the most expensive to the cheapest, that order would be: 10.__

    A. Novel, statistical, biography
    B. Statistical, biography, novel
    C. Biography, novel, statistical
    D. Statistical, novel, biography
    E. Biography, statistical, novel

11. How many books cost under $30?   11.__

    A. 2   B. 3   C. 4   D. 5   E. 6 or more

12. For which type(s) of books are the prices arranged so that the regular version could be the average in price of the prices of the condensed and expanded versions?

    A. Only novels   B. Only biographies
    C. Only statistical   D. Exactly 2 types
    E. All 3 types

12.____

13. For which type(s) of books are the prices arranged so that the condensed version costs MORE than the expanded version?

    A. All 3 types   B. Exactly 2 types
    C. Only biographies   D. Only novels
    E. None

13.____

14. Suppose that next year the cost of the condensed statistical book doubled, but all other prices remained the same.
Which statement(s) is(are) CORRECT?
    I. The condensed statistical book would be the most expensive.
    II. The price of the condensed statistical book would equal the price of the expanded novel book.
    III. The price of the condensed statistical book would exceed that of the expanded statistical book.
The CORRECT answer is:

    A. I *only*   B. II *only*
    C. III *only*   D. None of the above
    E. Exactly 2 of the above

14.____

Questions 15-22.

DIRECTIONS: Questions 15 through 22 are to be answered on the basis of the following set of facts.

Ann, Beth, Carol, Diane, and Eve have entered a local beauty contest in which Mr. Brown, Mr. Smith, and Mr. Jones are the judges. The point system to be used is 0, 1, 2, 3, and 4, where 4 is the highest. Each judge will rank each applicant exactly once, and no judges may assign the same ranking to two or more applicants. The girl with the highest total wins the contest. Brown and Jones both ranked Diane the same, and this ranking matched the score that Smith gave to Carol. Smith's ranking for Ann was exactly double Jones' ranking for Ann, but less than the score Brown assigned to Ann. Brown ranked Eve higher than Ann. Carol accumulated the same number of points as Ann. Carol and Ann were the only applicants who received three different rankings from the three judges.

15. Who won the contest?

    A. Ann   B. Beth   C. Carol   D. Diane   E. Eve

15.____

16. If the rules were adjusted so that for each applicant only the best two rankings given by the three judges would count, who would have the HIGHEST total?

    A. Ann   B. Beth   C. Carol   D. Diane   E. Eve

16.____

17. What is the complete list of applicants who did NOT receive any 0 rating?   17.___

    A. Ann, Carol, Diane   B. Ann, Beth, Eve
    C. Beth, Carol, Eve   D. Ann, Diane, Eve
    E. Beth, Carol, Diane

18. Who came in second place?   18.___

    A. Ann   B. Beth   C. Carol   D. Diane   E. Eve

19. Which judge(s) scored Diane the LOWEST?   19.___

    A. Only Brown   B. Only Jones
    C. Only Smith   D. Exactly 2 of them
    E. All 3 judges

20. Which judge(s) scored Ann the HIGHEST?   20.___

    A. Only Brown   B. Only Jones
    C. Only Smith   D. Exactly 2 of them
    E. None of them

21. How many applicants earned the HIGHEST ranking at least once?   21.___

    A. All 5   B. 4   C. 3   D. 2   E. 1

22. Which is(are) correct?   22.___
      I. Ann's total + Diane's total = Carol's total
      II. Beth's total + Diane's total = Ann's total
      III. Carol's total + Diane's total = Beth's total
  The CORRECT answer is:

    A. I *only*   B. II *only*   C. III *only*
    D. All of them   E. None of them

Questions 23-25.

DIRECTIONS: Questions 23 through 25 are based on the following paragraph.

There are 200 correctional facilities nationwide. Exactly 75% of all inmates with the disease AIDS are housed in correctional facilities in just three states: New Jersey, New York, and Pennsylvania. Also, 4% of the entire nation's correctional institutions have 72% of all the inmate AIDS cases; 50% of all such institutions are totally free of the disease.

23. How many AIDS-infected inmates are housed *outside* the states of New York, New Jersey, and Pennsylvania?   23.___

    A. 8   B. 25   C. 50   D. 75   E. 100

24. If one could find a total of 216 inmates with AIDS in just eight institutions, then the LEAST number of AIDS-infected inmates nationwide would be   24.___

    A. 240   B. 270   C. 300   D. 330   E. 360

25. It is a certainty that exactly _____ correctional facilities combined would contribute 28%   25.____
    of the total number of inmates with AIDS, where none of these institutions are disease-
    free.

    A. 46   B. 50   C. 72   D. 92   E. 100

_____

KEY (CORRECT ANSWERS)

1.	B		11.	C
2.	C		12.	B
3.	E		13.	E
4.	D		14.	C
5.	D		15.	E
6.	E		16.	E
7.	B		17.	B
8.	E		18.	B
9.	D		19.	D
10.	A		20.	E

21.	D
22.	C
23.	C
24.	C
25.	D

_____

SOLUTIONS TO PROBLEMS

For Questions 1 through 7, the order of towns from west to east are: Beta, Alpha, Gamma, Delta, and would be arranged mileage wise as:

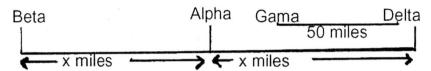

The present maximum speed limits are:
  Beta = 20 m.p.h.   Alpha = 60 m.p.h.
  Delta = 70 m.p.h.   Gamma = 75 m.p.h. or 80 m.p.h.

For Questions 8 through 14, the correct sequence in order of increasing price would be:

  Condensed biography, condensed novel, regular biography, expanded biography, regular novel, condensed statistical, regular statistical, expanded statistical, expanded novel.

There are three possible sets of solutions for the prices:

  1st solution: $5, $10, $15, $25, $30, $35, $40, $50, $75
  2nd solution: $5, $10, $20, $25, $30, $35, $40, $50, $75
  3rd solution: $5, $15, $20, $25, $30, $35, $40, $50, $75

Note that the differences occurred only in the lowest three prices.

  For Questions 15 through 22, the scoring by each judge and for each applicant appears as:

	Ann	Beth	Carol	Diane	Eve
Brown	3	1	2	0	4
Jones	1	3	4	0	2
Smith	2	3	0	1	4

23. 100% - 75% = 25% of AIDS-infected inmates are located outside the 3 states of New York, New Jersey, and Pennsylvania. (25%)(200) = 50. (Ans. C)

24. Eight institutions could represent the 4% of the entire nation's correctional facilities which have 72% of all inmate AIDS cases (200 times 4% =8). If 216 represents 72% of all such infected inmates, then the total number of AIDS-infected inmates is 216 ÷ 72% = 300. (Ans. C)

25. 100% - 4% - 50% = 46%, which could contribute 28% of the total number of inmates with AIDS. This 46% figure would represent the fraction of institutions outside the 4% and outside the 50% (which have no such cases). (46%)(200) = 92. (Ans. D)

ANALYTICAL REASONING

COMMENTARY

This unique type of question focuses on the ability to understand a structure of relationships and to draw conclusions about that structure. The examinee is asked to understand the conditions used to establish the structure of the relationship and to deduce new information from them. Each group of questions consists of (1) a set of several related conditions (and sometimes other explanatory material) describing a structure of relationships, and (2) three or more questions that test understanding of the implications of that structure. Although each question in a group is based on the same set of conditions, the questions are independent of one another; answering one question in a group does not depend on answering any other question.

Each group of questions is based on a set of conditions that establish relationships among persons, places, things, or events. The relationships are common ones such as temporal order

> (A arrived before B but after C);spatial order
> (X always sits in front of Y and behind Z);
> group membership (If Professor Smith serves on
> the committee, then Professor Jones must also
> serve); and family structure (Jane is John's
> mother and Beth's sister).

The conditions should be read carefully to determine the exact nature of the relationships involved. Some relationships are fixed (J and K always sit at the same table). Other relationships are variable (S must be assigned to either table 1 or table 3). Some relationships that are not stated in the conditions can be deduced from those that are stated (if one condition about books on a shelf specifies that Book M is to the left of Book N, and another specifies that Book O is to the left of Book M then it can be deduced that Book O is to the left of Book N.)

No knowledge of formal logic is required for solving these problems. These questions are intended to be answered using knowledge, skills, and reasoning ability which are expected of college students and graduates.

SUGGESTED APPROACH

Some persons may prefer to answer first those questions in a group that seem to pose little difficulty and then to return to those that seem troublesome. It is best not to start one group before finishing another because much time can be lost in returning to a question group and reestablishing familiarity with its relationships. Do not assume that, because the conditions for a set look long or complicated, the questions based on those conditions will be especially difficult.

In reading the conditions, do not introduce unwarranted assumptions; for instance, in a set establishing relationships of height and weight among the members of a team, do not assume that a person who is taller than another person must weigh more than that person.

It is intended that the conditions be as clear as possible; do not interpret them as if they were designed to trick you. For example, if a question asks how many people could be eligible to serve on a committee, consider only those people named in the explanatory material unless directed otherwise. When in doubt, read the conditions in their most obvious sense. However, the language in the conditions is intended to be read for precise meaning. It is essential, for instance, to pay particular attention to words that describe or limit relationships, such as *only, exactly, never, always, must be, cannot be,* and the like. The result of the careful reading described above should be a clear picture of the structure of relationships involved, including what kinds of relationships are permitted, who or what the participants in the relationships are, and what is and is not known about the structure of the relationships. For instance, following a careful reading it can often be determined whether only a single configuration of relationships is permitted by the conditions or whether alternative configurations are permitted.

Each question should be considered separately from the other questions in its group; no information, except what is given in the original conditions, should be carried over from one question to another. In some cases a question will simply ask for conclusions to be drawn from the conditions as originally given. An individual question can, however, add information to the original conditions or temporarily suspend one of the original conditions for the purpose of that question only. For example, if Question 1 adds the information "if P is setting at table 2 ....," this information should NOT be carried over to any other question in the group.

Many people find it useful to underline key points in the conditions.

As the directions for this type of question suggest, it may prove very helpful to draw a diagram representing the configuration to assist you in answering the question.

Even though some people find diagrams to be very helpful, other people seldom use them. And among those who do regularly use diagrams in solving these problems, there is by no means universal agreement on which kind of diagram is best for which problem or in which cases a diagram is most useful. Therefore, do not be concerned if a particular problem in the test seems to be best approached without the use of diagrams.

EXAMINATION SECTION
TEST 1

DIRECTIONS: Each question or incomplete statement is followed by several suggested answers or completions. Select the one that BEST answers the question or completes the statement. *PRINT THE LETTER OF THE CORRECT ANSWER IN THE SPACE AT THE RIGHT.*

QUESTIONS 1-7.

Questions 1-7 pertain to the following.

Five people, named Alice, Bob, Conrad, Diane, and Elaine are applying for jobs at the EZ Manufacturing Company. When they arrive at the personnel office, each will be assigned to a room to take a written test. The available rooms are numbered 1 through 6 and are arranged in numbered sequence from left to right along one side of a corridor. Certain restrictions shall apply.
1.   A maximum of 2 people may occupy the same room.
2.   Two females may NOT occupy the same room, except Alice and Elaine.
3.   Two men must NOT occupy adjacent rooms, nor may they occupy the same room.
4.   Alice and Bob used to be husband and wife. Thus, they refuse to be assigned to either the same room or to adjacent rooms.
5.   Conrad and Diane are engaged and want to be assigned to either the same room or to adjacent rooms.
6.   There must be at least 1 vacant room next to Elaine's room.

1.   If each person is assigned to a different room, which of the following is(are) acceptable arrangement(s) for rooms 1 through 6 respectively?
    I.   Alice, Diane, Bob, Conrad, Elaine, Vacant
    II.   Vacant, Elaine, Bob, Diane, Conrad, Alice
    III.   Bob, Elaine, Vacant, Conrad, Alice, Diane
The CORRECT answer is:

    A.   I only
    D.   None
    B.   II only
    E.   I, II, and III
    C.   III only

1.____

2.   Suppose Diane and Elaine are taking the same test and are directed to rooms 1 and 6 respectively.
If Bob is assigned to room 3, which of the following is TRUE?

    A.   Alice can be assigned to room 4
    B.   Conrad can be assigned either to room 1 or to room 2
    C.   Alice and Conrad will share adjacent rooms
    D.   Room 4 must be vacant
    E.   Conrad must be assigned to room 1

2.____

3.   Consider the conditions presented in the previous question. Which of the following is a complete and accurate list of the room(s) which could be simultaneously vacant?

    A.   Room 2 *only*
    D.   Rooms 4 and 5
    B.   Rooms 2 and 4
    E.   Rooms 2, 4, and 5
    C.   Room 5 *only*

3.____

4. Suppose the first room is occupied by Conrad and Diane, the second room is vacant, and the third room is occupied by Elaine.
   If the fourth room is not vacant, then which of the following situations MUST be false?

   A. The fifth room is vacant
   B. Bob is assigned to the sixth room
   C. Alice is assigned to the fourth room
   D. Bob is assigned to the fifth room
   E. None of the above

   4.___

5. Alice is assigned to room 1, Elaine to room 3, and Bob to room 4.
   In how many different ways can Diane and Conrad be assigned to rooms?

   A. 1   B. 2   C. 3   D. 4   E. 5 or more

   5.___

6. Based on the conditions in the previous question, which room(s) must be vacant?

   A. Room 2   B. Rooms 5 and 6   C. Room 5 or room 6
   D. Room 6   E. Rooms 2 and 5

   6.___

7. If Bob is assigned to room 5, which of the following is a complete list of people who CAN-NOT be assigned to room 6?

   A. Alice and Elaine   B. Diane and Elaine
   C. Diane and Conrad   D. Diane, Conrad, and Elaine
   E. Alice, Diane, and Elaine

   7.___

QUESTIONS 8-12.

Questions 8-12 pertain to the following conditions.

Four people, Ginny, Harry, Ike, and June, are running in a one mile race along a straight roadway. After exactly 2 minutes, a photograph of all 4 runners is taken. We find out that
   1. Ginny is 20 yards ahead of Harry.
   2. Harry and Ike are 10 yards apart.
   3. June is 5 yards behind Ike.

8. Who must be in *second* place?

   A. Either Harry or Ike   B. Either Harry or June
   C. Ike   D. June
   E. Either Ike or June

   8.___

9. What is the MINIMAL distance, in yards, between Ginny and the runner immediately behind her?

   A. 5   B. 10   C. 15
   D. 20   E. it cannot be determined

   9.___

10. The distance between the 3rd and 4th place runners must be

   A. less than 5 yards
   B. 5 yards
   C. more than 5 yards but less than 10 yards
   D. 10 yards
   E. more than 10 yards

   10.___

11. The distance between the 2 females is _____ yards.   11._____

    A.   10   B.   15   C.   Either 15 or 30
    D.   Either 10 or 30   E.   More than 30

12. The longest distance separates which 2 *consecutive* runners?   12._____

    A.   Harry and Ike
    B.   Harry and June or Ike and June
    C.   Harry and June
    D.   Ike and June or Ginny and Ike
    E.   Ginny and Harry or Ginny and Ike

QUESTIONS 13-19.

Questions 13-19 pertain to the following conditions.

From the Happy Landing Airport, 3 different airlines operate; Algebraic Airlines, Calculus Airlines, and Geometric Airlines. These airlines have flights both into and out of the airport. Assume that a plane is always available for each airline when needed. Certain restrictions apply.

    1.   The airport is open continuously except between 11:05 PM and 1:55 AM, inclusive.
    2.   Algebraic planes leave from landing strip 1 and arrive at strip 3.
    3.   Calculus planes depart from strip 2 and arrive at landing strip 1.
    4.   Geometric planes leave from strip 3 and can arrive at either strip 2 or strip 3.
    5.   In the interest of safety, no 2 planes may either arrive at or depart from the same landing strip unless their times are at least 10 minutes apart.
    6.   If 2 planes are utilizing 2 different landing strips, their times of either arrival or departure must be at least 10 minutes apart.
    7.   For Algebraic Airlines, planes leave once an hour at 10 minutes after the hour. Their arriving planes reach the airport 4 times each day. Arrival times are 3:00 AM, 6:00 AM, 9:00 AM and 12:00 Noon.
    8.   Calculus planes leave twice an hour -- at 5 minutes after and before the hour. Arrivals are at 2:00 AM, 10:00 AM, and 6:00 PM.
    9.   Geometric planes leave randomly but must depart 3 times each hour, counting from on the hour. Their planes arrive randomly once every 2 hours counting from on the hour, when the airport is first opened each day.

13. Between 3:05 PM and 5:05 PM inclusive, what is the number of planes which either   13._____
arrive at or leave from strip 3 that belong to Geometric Airlines?

    A.   8   B.   9   C.   More than 8
    D.   At most 8   E.   More than 9

14. Between 3:05 AM and 6:05 AM inclusive, how many arriving planes are there at landing   14._____
strip 3?

    A.   1   B.   2   C.   At most 2
    D.   2 or 3   E.   More than 3

15. Which airline utilizes all 3 landing strips?   15.____

    A. Algebraic   B. Geometric
    C. Calculus   D. Exactly 2 of the airlines
    E. None of the airlines

16. A Calculus plane has just landed in the early evening. What is the number of Calculus   16.____
planes which will depart from the airport between 6:00 PM and 6:55 PM, inclusive?

    A. 1   B. 2   C. 3   D. 4   E. 5

17. What is the MAXIMUM number of planes which may depart between 1:20 PM and 2:30   17.____
PM, inclusive?

    A. 4   B. 5   C. 6   D. 7   E. 8

18. It is now 5:17 PM. A traffic controller has noticed that since 5:00 PM, exactly two Geo-   18.____
metric planes have departed. He also has noticed that the next Geometric plane is due to
arrive at strip 3 at 5:58 PM.
What is the latest time, of the following, before 6:00 PM, when another Geometric
plane will depart?

    A. 5:20 PM   B. 5:25 PM   C. 5:30 PM   D. 5:45 PM   E. 5:55 PM

19. A plane has departed from landing strip 2 exactly 15 minutes ago.   19.____
What is the MINIMUM time that must elapse before a Geometric plane can arrive at
the airport?

    A. 10 minutes   B. 15 minutes   C. 30 minutes
    D. 45 minutes   E. 1 hour

QUESTIONS 20-25.

Questions 20-25 pertain to the following conditions.

There are four people standing on a flight of 4 steps. The following restrictions apply:
1. No more than two people may stand on any one step.
2. Allen and David can neither be on the same step nor on 2 adjacent steps.
3. Beth and Connie must be either on the same step or on 2 adjacent steps.
4. David MUST not occupy the same step with anyone.
5. Allen will never occupy step 4.

20. If Allen is on step 1 and David is on step 3, in how many different ways can Beth and   20.____
Connie be assigned to the steps?

    A. 2   B. 3   C. 4   D. 5   E. 6

21. Which of the following conditions would imply that each person occupies a different step?   21.____

    A. David is on step 4; Beth, Allen, Connie are on different steps
    B. Beth is on step 2; Connie is on step 3
    C. Allen is on step 3; Connie is on step 2
    D. Allen and Beth are on different steps
    E. Neither Beth nor Connie is on step 4

22. Which of the following conditions is NOT allowed?   22.____

    A. Allen on step 1
    B. Allen and Beth both on step 1
    C. Step 1 being vacant
    D. Connie on step 4
    E. David on step 2

23. Which of the following conditions would imply that step 2 is vacant?   23.____

    A. Beth and Connie both on step 4
    B. Allen and Beth both on step 3
    C. Allen and Connie both on step 4
    D. David on step 1
    E. None of the above

24. If Beth and Connie choose to be on different steps, which numbered step(s) could be 24.____
    vacant?

    A. Steps 1 and 4   B. Steps 2 and 3   C. Only step 2
    D. Any 2 steps   E. Any 2 step

25. What is the complete list of individuals who are eligible to occupy step 1 if step 3 must be 25.____
    vacant?

    A. Allen, David
    B. Allen, Beth, Connie
    C. Beth, Connie, David
    D. Beth, Connie
    E. Allen, Beth, Connie, David

KEY (CORRECT ANSWERS)

1.	B	11.	C
2.	E	12.	E
3.	E	13.	D
4.	D	14.	D
5.	B	15.	E
6.	A	16.	B
7.	D	17.	E
8.	A	18.	D
9.	B	19.	A
10.	B	20.	C

21.	A
22.	E
23.	A
24.	E
25.	B

SOLUTIONS TO PROBLEMS

1. Selection I violates conditions 3 and 5. Selection III violates condition 5.

(Answer B)

2. Alice would have to be assigned to room 6, so as not to violate any conditions. Room 5 must remain vacant in order to comply with condition 6. By condition 3, Conrad may not occupy rooms 2, 3, or 4, But condition 5 then implies that Conrad be assigned to room 1.

(Answer E)

3. Room 5 is already vacant. Rooms 2 and 4 can also be vacant by the following assignment: Conrad and Diane to room 1, Bob to room 3, Alice and Elaine to room 6.

(Answer E)

4. Choices A, B, and C could be true with the assignment of Alice and Bob to the 4th and 6th rooms respectively. However, if Bob were placed in room 5, there would be no place to put Alice without violating condition 4.

(Answer D)

5. By condition 6, room 2 must be vacant. Condition 3 forces Conrad to be assigned to room 6. Since Diane and Conrad must be either in the same room or in adjacent rooms, she can be in room 5 or room 6. Thus, either Diane and Conrad are both in room 6, or they are in rooms 5 and 6, respectively.

(Answer B)

6. As described above, room 5 may be vacant, But not necessarily if Diane is in room 5 and Conrad in room 6. Only room 2 MUST be vacant.

(Answer A)

7. Condition 6 prohibits Elaine from being assigned to room 6. By condition 3, Conrad could only be assigned to rooms 1, 2, or 3. Condition 5 would thus restrict Diane to rooms 1, 2, 3, or 4.

(Answer D)

8. The photograph will show one of 2 scenes for the identity of the runners in 1st through last place respectively.
    Scene 1: Ginny, Ike, June, Harry.
    Scene 2: Ginny, Harry, Ike, June.
    Thus, either Harry or Ike is in 2nd place.

(Answer A)

9. For scene 1, the distances between the 1st and 2nd runners, 2nd and 3rd, 3rd and 4th are 10 yards, 5 yards, and 5 yards respectively. The corresponding distances for scene 2 are 20 yards, 10 yards, and 5 yards respectively. Thus, scene 1 shows only a distance of 10 yards separating Ginny and the 2nd place runner (Ike).

(Answer B)

10.   For either scene, 5 yards separate the 3rd and 4th place runners.

(Answer B)

11.   In scene 1, Ginny and 3rd place June are 15 yards apart. But in scene 2, June is in last place, and now is 30 yards behind Ginny.

(Answer C)

12.   For scene 1, the biggest gap is between Ginny and Ike. In scene 2, the largest gap is the 20 yards between Ginny and Harry.

(Answer E)

13.   By condition 9, a total of 7 Geometric planes will depart from strip 3: 3 between 3:05 and 4:00, 3 between 4:00 and 5:00, and 1 plane between 5:00 and 5:05. Now. from 3:00 to 5:00, 1 Geometric plane must leave. Also,it is IMPOSSIBLE that a Geometric plane will leave between 5:00 and 5:05 under the condition that 1 plane has already arrived during this interval. This would conflict with restriction 5. Thus, at most 8 Geometric plane are involved.

(Answer D)

14.   1 Algebraic plane will arrive at 6:00 AM and 1 Geometric plane must arrive between 3:00 and 5:00. Additionally, one more Geometric plane must arrive at either strip 2 or 3 between 5:00 and 7:00; thus, it could arrive at strip 3 by 6:05.

(Answer D)

15.   By inspecting the given conditions, each airline is found to be using exactly 2 airstrips.

(Answer E)

16.   The 2 Calculus planes will leave at 6:05 PM and 6:55 PM.

(Answer B)

17.   An Algebraic plane will depart at 2:10. 3 Geometric planes will depart between 1:20 and 1:50 and 2 more Geometric planes can leave at 2:20 and 2:30. Now, 2 Calculus planes will depart at 1:55 and 2:05. Note that due to restriction 6, no more Geometric planes may be allowed to depart. Total of 8 planes maximum.

(Answer E)

18.   A Geometric plane could depart as late as 5:45 but no later, since a Calculus plane will leave at 5:55.

(Answer D)

19.   Conditions 5 and 6 both require that a minimum of 10 minutes must elapse between arrival/departing times of any planes.

(Answer A)

20. The 4 possibilities are:
    1. Beth and Connie both on step 2.
    2. Beth on step 1, Connie on step 2.
    3. Beth on step 2, Connie on step 1.
    4. Beth and Connie both on step 4.

(Answer C)

21. Since David shares his step with no one, CHOICE A yields the arrangement of Allen, Beth, Connie, David (Beth and Connie may be interchanged). For CHOICE B, it can be refuted by placing Allen on step 2. CHOICE C can be refuted with Beth and Connie both on step 2, David on step 1, and Allen on step 3. Also, CHOICES D and E can be refuted by the arrangement mentioned in the last sentence.

(Answer A)

22. With David on step 2, there is no place left for Allen, since condition 2 forbids Allen from steps 1, 2, or 3 and condition 5 forbids him from step 4.
    CHOICES A, B, C, and D are permissible.

(Answer E)

23. If Beth and Connie are both on step 4, then Allen and David are BOTH restricted to steps 1, 2, and 3 (Condition 1). Since the two men cannot be on adjacent steps or the same step, one of them will occupy step 1 and the other will occupy step 3.

(Answer A)

24. For step 1 vacant: Allen and Beth on step 2, Connie on step 3, David on step 4.
    For step 2 vacant: David on step 1, Allen and Connie on step 3, Beth on step 4
    For step 3 vacant: Connie on step 1, Allen and Beth on step 2, David on step 4.
    For step 4 vacant: David on step 1, Beth on step 2, Allen and Connie on step 3.
    Note that no 2 steps could be vacant simultaneously.

(Answer E)

25. Possible arrangements are: 1. Beth and Connie on step 1, Allen on step 2, David on step 4; 2. Allen on step 1, Beth and Connie on step 2, David on step 4; David would not be allowed on step 1, since there is no place to put Allen.

(Answer B)

EXAMINATION SECTION
TEST 1

DIRECTIONS: Each question or incomplete statement is followed by several suggested answers or completions. Select the one that BEST answers the question or completes the statement. *PRINT THE LETTER OF THE BEST ANSWER IN THE SPACE AT THE RIGHT.*

QUESTIONS 1-5.

Questions 1-5 pertain to the following.

The Know-Z Marketing Company is interested in determining the major sports preferences of a large city. A total of 100 people are sent a questionnaire on which the sports of baseball, basketball, and football are listed. Each respondent is asked to place a check mark next to each sport he likes. When the 100 responses were received, the following results emerged:

1. Five individuals showed a preference for all 3 sports.
2. Some individuals liked no sport.
3. Ten people liked basketball and football, but not baseball.
4. A total of 40 individuals checked off football.
5. Eighteen people showed a preference for only basketball.
6. A total of twenty-four people checked off exactly 2 sports.
7. A total of 50 people showed a preference for only one sport.

1. How many people checked off *both* basketball and football? 1.____
   A. 5   B. 10   C. 15   D. 20   E. 25

2. If 16 people preferred only football, how many people preferred baseball and basketball, but NOT football? 2.____
   A. 5   B. 10   C. 15   D. 20   E. 25

3. Suppose no responses were received on which both baseball and basketball but not football were checked off. How many individuals did NOT check off basketball? 3.____
   A. 30   B. 46   C. 53   D. 67   E. 72

4. Suppose 6 people checked off baseball and football, but not basketball. How many respondents checked off *both* baseball and basketball? 4.____
   A. 8   B. 10   C. 13   D. 15   E. 18

5. What is the MINIMUM number of people who checked off basketball? 5.____
   A. 5   B. 10   C. 18   D. 23   E. 33

QUESTIONS 6-11.

Questions 6-11 pertain to the following.

The Liftweight elevator is capable of carrying up to and including 550 lbs. The six individuals who use this elevator, and their respective weights are: Adam, 200 lbs.; Bonnie, 125 lbs.; Cathy, 150 lbs.; David, 175 lbs.; Eva, 100 lbs.; and Frank, 250 lbs.

The following restrictions exist:
1. Frank will not ride alone.
2. Bonnie will only ride the elevator if either Cathy or Eva is also a passenger. However, Bonnie will not ride with both of these ladies simultaneously.
3. David will either ride alone or with at least one of the ladies.
4. Adam will ride the elevator only if the total weight of the other passenger(s) is between 100 lbs. and 200 lbs, inclusive.

6. If Adam is on the elevator, which of the following is(are) permissible?   6.___
    I.   David is the only other passenger.
    II. Cathy is the only other passenger.
    III. Frank is the only other passenger.
The CORRECT answer is:

    A. I only   B. II only   C. III only
    D. I, II only   E. I, II, and III

7. Frank, Bonnie, and Eva are currently on the elevator, heading toward the first floor. On   7.___
the way down, the elevator stops at the second floor, where David is waiting to board. Which one of the following actions is NOT allowed?

    A. Bonnie steps out and David steps into the elevator
    B. Eva steps out and David steps into the elevator
    C. Frank steps out and David steps into the elevator
    D. Both Frank and Bonnie step out and David does not step into the elevator
    E. Frank, Bonnie, and Eva step out and David steps into the elevator

8. How many of these 6 individuals can ride alone?   8.___

    A. none   B. 1   C. 2   D. 3   E. 4 or more

9. Adam and Eva are riding the elevator as it approaches the 5th floor, and neither of them   9.___
intends to exit at that floor. If the other 4 people are waiting on the 5th floor, how many combinations exist for those who may join Adam and Eva as passengers?

    A. none   B. 1 or 2
    C. 3 or 4   D. 5 or 6
    E. more than 6

10. Which of the following is the MOST complete and accurate list of passengers who may   10.___
NOT share the elevator ride with both Eva and Bonnie simultaneously?

    A. David   B. Cathy and Frank
    C. Adam   D. Frank and David
    E. Adam and Cathy

11. If it is known that the weight of all individuals on the elevator is exactly 400 lbs. and if   11.___
none of the original 4 restrictions existed, how many combinations of individuals could ride the elevator?

    A. 1   B. 2   C. 3   D. 4   E. 5

QUESTIONS 12-16.

Questions 12-16 pertain to the following:

A blue box weighs one-half of a red box.
A green box weighs 3 lbs. more than a blue box.
A yellow box weighs the average of the weights of a green and red box.

12. Which color box is the heaviest?   12.____

    A. Blue   B. Green   C. Red or yellow
    D. Yellow or green   E. Green or red

13. Which color box is the lightest?   13.____

    A. Blue   B. Green   C. Red or blue
    D. Yellow or green   E. Green or red

14. If the blue box is 15 lbs. how much does the yellow box weigh?   14.____

    A. 12 lbs.   B. 18 lbs.   C. 21 lbs.   D. 24 lbs.   E. 30 lbs.

15. Suppose the red box is the 2nd lightest box.   15.____
    Then the green box must weight

    A. more than 6 lbs.
    B. more than 3 lbs.
    C. 3 lbs.
    D. between 3 lbs. and 6 lbs. inclusive
    E. less than 6 lbs.

16. If the yellow box weighs more than the green box, and the red box weighs 20 lbs., which   16.____
    of the following conclusions can be drawn about the yellow box? It weighs

    A. between 10 lbs. and 13 lbs. not inclusive
    B. between 13 lbs. and 20 lbs. not inclusive
    C. more than 20 lbs.
    D. less than 13 lbs.
    E. none of the above

QUESTIONS 17-22.

Questions 17-22 pertain to the following.

At the Studymore High School, a student is required to sign up for 6 classes during the 7 period school day. (No two classes may be taught during one period.) The following restrictions apply:
1. Language must be scheduled during an odd numbered period.
2. History must be scheduled during period 4, 5, or 6.
3. Mathematics must be scheduled at least 2 periods later than a Language class.
4. Science may only be scheduled between a Language class and a History class.
5. Economics can be scheduled for any even numbered period, but must not precede a mathematics class.
6. Art must be scheduled during period 1, 2, 6, or 7.
7. No more than 4 classes may be scheduled consecutively.

17. What is the complete list of periods which could be vacant?   17.___

   A. 3 *only*   B. 4 *only*   C. 3 or 5   D. 4 or 5   E. 3, 4, or 5

18. If art is scheduled during period 6, then which course could be scheduled during period 7?   18.___

   A. Language   B. Science   C. Economics
   D. History   E. None of these

19. What is the complete list of courses which may NOT be offered during period 1?   19.___

   A. Language, History, Economics. Science
   B. Mathematics, History, Science, Economics, Art
   C. Language, Science, History, Mathematics
   D. Mathematics, Science, Economics
   E. Mathematics, History, Science, Art

20. If period 4 is vacant, which is the CORRECT sequence of classes for periods 1, 2, and 3 respectively?   20.___

   A. Language, Art, Science   B. Language, Art, Mathematics
   C. Art, Science, Language   D. Language, Science, Mathematics
   E. Art, Science, Mathematics

21. If History is scheduled for period 4, in how many ways can the other 5 courses be scheduled?   21.___

   A. 1   B. 2   C. 3   D. 4   E. at least 5

22. If Mathematics is offered during period 3, then period 6 will be scheduled with   22.___

   A. Science   B. Science or History
   C. Economics   D. Economics or Science
   E. Economics or History

QUESTIONS 23-25.

Questions 23-25 pertain to the following:

The town of Petville allows each household to own a maximum of 2 dogs, 4 cats, and 5 birds.

23. If the Adams family has at least 2 of each of these 3 types of pets, how many different combinations of numbers of each type of pet would there be?   23.____

   A. 3   B. 6   C. 12   D. 20   E. 40

24. The Smith family has no dogs, but has more cats than birds. What is the MAXIMUM number of pets in this household?   24.____

   A. 9   B. 7   C. 6   D. 4   E. 3

25. The Jones family has fewer cats than either dogs or birds. Also, the number of birds does not exceed the number of birds in the Smith family in the preceding question. What is the MAXIMUM number of pets in the Jones family?   25.____

   A. 10   B. 9   C. 8   D. 7   E. 6

KEY (CORRECT ANSWERS)

1.	C		11.	B
2.	A		12.	E
3.	B		13.	A
4.	C		14.	D
5.	E		15.	E
6.	B		16.	B
7.	B		17.	E
8.	D		18.	E
9.	A		19.	B
10.	E		20.	D

21.	A
22.	E
23.	C
24.	B
25.	E

SOLUTIONS TO PROBLEMS

For Questions 1-5 consider this diagram:

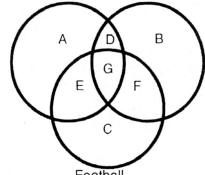

Baseball   Basketball

The letters represent number corresponding to those areas.

Football

Using the information in conditions 1, 3, and 5, we know: G=5, F=10, and B=18.

Condition 2 implies that A + B + ... + G < 100.
Condition 4 implies C + E + F + G = 40 or C + E = 25.
Condition 6 implies D + E + F = 24 or D + E = 14.
Condition 7 implies A + B + C = 50 or A + C = 32.

1. We seek F + G = 10 + 5 = 15

(Answer C)

2. Since we are given that C = 16, condition 4 would result in E = 9. Finally, condition 6 gives D + 9 = 14, or D = 5.

(Answer A)

3. Supposing D = 0, we can find A + C + D + E by adding the equations for conditions 6 and 7. (Note that D = 0 does not affect the answer.)

(Answer B)

4. Since E = 6, condition 6 gives D = 8. Thus D + G = 8 + 5 = 13.

(Answer C)

5. Regardless of the value of D, B + F + G = 18 + 10 + 5 = 33.

(Answer E)

6. If David and Adam were the only passengers, condition 3 would be violated. If Frank and Adam were passengers, condition 4 would be violated. Only Cathy may be the other passenger.

(Answer B)

7. If the elevator contained Frank, Bonnie, and David, then condition 2 would be violated.

(Answer B)

8. Only Cathy, Eva, or David could ride alone. If any of the others rode alone, restriction 1, 2, or 4 would be violated.

(Answer D)

9. Restriction 4 restricts the weights of the other passengers to a limit of 200 lbs. When Eva stays on as a passenger, only 100 more lbs. would be allowed. However, all other riders exceed 100 lbs.

(Answer A)

10. If Adam joins Eva and Bonnie, the 4th condition is out. If Cathy joins the 2 ladies, condition 2 is violated.

(Answer E)

11. The two combinations would be: a) Eva, Bonnie, David; and b) Bonnie, Frank.

(Answer B)

For Questions 12-16, the increasing order of weights is either blue, green, yellow, red or blue, red, yellow, green.

12. Self explanatory from above sentence.

(Answer E)

13. Self explanatory from above sentence.

(Answer A)

14. The red box is 30 lbs., green box is 18 lbs., and the yellow box is the average of 18 and 30, which is 24 lbs.

(Answer D)

15. This implies that the green box is the heaviest. If x = weight of the blue box, $2x$ = weight of the red box, $x + 3$ = weight of the green box, then we must have $2x < x + 3$ or $x < 3$ (i.e., blue box is less than 3 lbs.) Thus, the green box will be less than 6 lbs.

(Answer E)

16. The order is blue, green, yellow, red (increasing weight). We know the blue box is 10 lbs. (half the red box), and the green box is 3 lbs. more than the blue box or 13 lbs. Finally, the yellow box must be the average of 13 and 20 or 16 1/2 lbs.

(Answer B)

For Questions 17-22, the original schedule might appear as follows (using the L = Language, M = Mathematics, H = History, E = Economics, A = Art, S = Science).

Period #	1	2	3	4	5	6	7
	L		L		L		L
		M	M	M	M	M	M
			H	H	H		
		S	S	S			
				E		E	
	A	A				A	A

When all restrictions have been considered, certain options drop out and the final distribution appreas as:

Period #	1	2	3	4	5	6	7
	L	S	M	M	M	M	A
				H	H	H	
				E		E	

(Keep in mind that one period will be vacant.)

17. If any of periods 1, 2, 6, or 7 were vacant, restriction 7 is out.

(Answer E)

18. By the first diagram above and all restrictions considered, all periods 1 through 6 would have to have the classes Language, Science, Mathematics, Economics, History, Art, Vacant. Again, restriction 7 is being violated.

(Answer E)

19. The 2nd diagram shows only language being offered in period 1.

(Answer B)

20. Answer is evident from 2nd diagram.

(Answer D)

21. The only single combination is: Language, Science, Mathematics, History, Vacant, Economics, Art.

(Answer A)

22. The combinations allowed, where _____ = vacant are:
    a) L, S, M, _____, H, E, A; or
    b) L, S, M, E, _____, H, A.

(Answer E)

23. The family has 2 dogs, either 2, 3, or 4 cats and either 2, 3, 4, or 5 birds. The number of combinations = the product of the number of different numbers of each pet. Thus 1 x 3 x 4 = 12. As an example, one combination for dogs, cats, and birds would be 2, 2, and 4 respectively. Another might be 2, 4, 3 respectively. There are 12 such arrangements.

(Answer C)

24. Maximum would be: 0 dogs, 4 cats, 3 birds = 7 pets.

(Answer B)

25. Since the maximum number of dogs is 2, the maximum number of cats is 1. Since the Smith Family had a maximum of 3 birds, the same goes for the Jones Family. Now 2 + 1 + 3 = 6 pets maximum.

(Answer E)

———

EXAMINATION SECTION
TEST 1

DIRECTIONS: Each question or incomplete statement is followed by several suggested answers or completions. Select the one that BEST answers the question or completes the statement. *PRINT THE LETTER OF THE CORRECT ANSWER IN THE SPACE AT THE RIGHT.*

QUESTIONS 1-5.

Questions 1-5 refer to the following:

The cruising speed of all of the following automobiles is in a number ending in the digit 5 or 0.
1. Ford has a cruising speed 15 m.p.h. above a Plymouth.
2. Chevy has a cruising speed 20 m.p.h. above a Ford.
3. Datsun has a cruising speed exactly one-half as great as a Ford, but is only 10 m.p.h. below a Plymouth.
4. Toyota has a cruising speed between that of a Plymouth and that of a Chevy, but greater than that of a Ford.

1. Which of the following is the CORRECT order of cruising speeds from *fastest* to *slowest*?   1._____

   A. Chevy, Ford, Plymouth, Toyota, Datsun
   B. Chevy, Toyota, Ford, Plymouth, Datsun
   C. Ford, Plymouth, Chevy, Toyota, Datsun
   D. Plymouth, Toyota, Chevy, Datsun, Ford
   E. Chevy, Ford, Toyota, Datsun, Plymouth

2. What is the cruising speed of a Chevy?   2._____

   A. Under 50 m.p.h.
   B. More than 50 m.p.h. but less than 65 m.p.h.
   C. 65 m.p.h.
   D. More than 65 m.p.h. but less than 70 m.p.h.
   E. 70 m.p.h.

3. In order for the Toyota's cruising speed to be *exactly* halfway between that of a Ford and that of a Chevy, it must be _____ m.p.h. faster than a Datsun.   3._____

   A. 15   B. 25   C. 35   D. 50   E. 60

4. If the cruising speed of a Plymouth were increased to twice its current speed, it would then exceed how many other autos?   4._____

   A. 2   B. 3   C. 4   D. 1   E. 0

5. Assume that the cruising speed of a Buick ends in the digit 0 or 5.   5._____
   If that speed is less than 3 times that of a Plymouth but at least 4 times that of a Datsun, then the Buick's speed is m.p.h.

   A. Either 105 or 110   B. 105 *only*
   C. 100 *only*   D. 110 *only*
   E. More than 110

QUESTIONS 6-10.

Questions 6-10 refer to the following.

In Deep Creek High School, Physical Education meets on Monday, Wednesday, and Friday during first period; and, Tuesday and Thursday during last period. Assume that first period is in the morning and that last period is in the afternoon. In order for a student to be excused from a Physical Education class, he must get a note from the School Nurse, bring an approval from a School Doctor, and obtain a permission of excusal from the Vice Principal. Certain additional restrictions apply:

1. The School Doctor is only available on Tuesday before school and on both Wednesday and Thursday after school.
2. The School Nurse is available on Monday and Wednesday before school but will not issue a note without the doctor's signature.
3. The Vice Principal is available only after school and only on days when the nurse is not available.
4. The Vice Principal will issue a permission for excusal only if both an approval from the doctor and a note from the nurse are also submitted.

6. On Monday morning, little Jimmy doesn't feel well.
   When is the earliest time that he can get excused from Physical Education class?

   A. Tuesday morning
   C. Wednesday morning
   E. Friday morning
   B. Tuesday afternoon
   D. Thursday afternoon

6.___

7. Referring to the facts in the preceding question, if the rule about seeing the Vice Principal were waived, when would be the earliest time for excusal?

   A. Tuesday morning
   C. Wednesday morning
   E. Thursday afternoon
   B. Tuesday afternoon
   D. Wednesday afternoon

7.___

8. Early Wednesday morning before school, Bobby becomes ill. The School Nurse is not in, but the nurse's aide is willing to give him a note. However, the doctor refuses to issue an approval until the following week.
   The earliest time that Bobby can be excused from Physical Education class under these circumstances is _____ of the following week.

   A. Monday morning
   C. Tuesday afternoon
   E. Wednesday afternoon
   B. Tuesday morning
   D. Wednesday morning

8.___

9. Johnny has just received a signed note from the Vice Principal, which will excuse him from Physical Education class. On this particular day, he did not receive a doctor's note or nurse's note, but he had received these two notes earlier in the week.
   This implies that Johnny received the Vice Principal's note _____.

   A. Wednesday
   C. Friday
   E. either Thursday or Friday
   B. Thursday
   D. either Wednesday or Thursday

9.___

10. If a student becomes ill on Monday after school, he could miss a Physical Education class as early as _____ if the 3 notes are received in ANY order.   10.____

    A. Tuesday morning   B. Tuesday afternoon
    C. Wednesday morning   D. Wednesday afternoon
    E. None of the above

QUESTIONS 11-15.

Questions 11-15 refer to the following:

On the radio dial of the newest type of radio, 100 AM corresponds to 150 FM, and 125 AM corresponds to 200 FM. Station W is to the left of station X, and are both on AM. Stations V, Y, and Z are all on FM, with Z lying between V and Y. It is also known that the call number for X is lower than the call number (station number) for Z. The call number for Y lies between the call numbers for W and X.

11. If a station had call number 110 AM, it would correspond to _____ FM.   11.____

    A. 160   B. 170
    C. 180   D. 190
    E. none of these

12. What is the CORRECT *ascending* order of stations with regard to their associated numbers? (Disregard whether AM or FM)   12.____

    A. WYXZV   B. WXYZV   C. WYZXV
    D. WYZVX   E. WXZVY

13. If W is call number 105 and Y is call number 120, what call number describes X?   13.____

    A. Higher than 115   B. Lower than 125
    C. Higher than 120   D. Between 100 and 125
    E. Lower than 115

14. Suppose X is call number 100 and Z is call number 180. Thus, when moving the dial from left to right, we can be certain that the AM call number correspnding to the location of V is _____.   14.____

    A. higher than 115   B. lower than 125
    C. higher than 100   D. between 100 and 125
    E. lower than 115

15. Suppose that, in moving the dial from left to right, the first 3 stations reached are Y, Z, and W, respectively. A new FM station P corresponds to the location of station W. If the call number for P is double that of Z, then the call number for W is _____.   15.____

    A. double that of Y   B. double that of Z
    C. 10 less than that of X   D. 25 more than that of Z
    E. more than double that of Y

QUESTIONS 16-19.

Questions 16-19 refer to the following:

At a business luncheon, there were four guest speakers: Robert, Sam, Ted, and Vic. Each speaker provided at least one business tip on how to be successful. It is also known that:

1. Robert spoke before Sam, but after Vic.
2. Ted was not the last speaker, but spoke after Robert.
3. Robert gave less than twice as many tips as Ted, but only one-third as many as Vic.
4. Ted did not give the fewest number of tips, but gave five fewer tips than Robert.
5. Sam gave exactly one-fourth as many tips as Rober.

16. The CORRECT order of speakers from *last to first* is: 16.___

   A. Vic, Ted, Robert, Sam   B. Sam, Robert, Ted, Vic
   C. Sam, Ted, Robert, Vic   D. Vic, Robert, Ted, Sam
   E. Robert, Sam, Ted, Vic

17. How many tips did Robert give? 17.___

   A. 8   B. 9   C. 10   D. 11   E. At least 12

18. Which of the following numbers could NOT represent the number of tips Vic gave? 18.___

   A. 33   B. 36   C. 39   D. 42   E. 45

19. If Vic had actually given *fewer* than 50 tips, then Ted would have given _____ tips. 19.___

   A. 15   B. 20
   C. 25   D. 30
   E. none of these

QUESTIONS 20-25.

Questions 20-25 refer to the following:

A dentist by the name of Dr. Toothclean has six patients in the waiting room with different appointment times. There are two men and four ladies. Unfortunately, he has misplaced his appointment book; but he does remember certain facts:
1. Each individual's appointment is either exactly on the hour or half-hour.
2. Mr. Pain's appointment is later than 1:00 PM but earlier than Miss Root's.
3. Mrs. Cavity's appointment is halfway between Miss Root's and Mr. Molar's.
4. Miss Novocaine's appointment is at 1:30 PM.
5. The time of Miss Injection's appointment is half as close to Miss Novocaine's as it is to Mr. Pain's time.
6. Mr. Molar's appointment is later than Mr. Pain's time.

20. What is the EARLIEST possible time for Miss Injection's appointment? 20.___

   A. 12:30 PM   B. 1:00 PM   C. 1:30 PM
   D. 2:00 PM   E. 2:30 PM

21. Of these 6 patients, who will be the THIRD patient to be attended to?   21.____

   A. Miss Novocaine   B. Miss Novocaine or Mr. Pain
   C. Miss Novocaine or Mr. Molar   D. Mr. Pain
   E. Mrs. Cavity

22. How many individuals have appointments before 1:00 PM?   22.____

   A. 0   B. 0 or 1   C. 1   D. 1 or 2   E. 2

23. How many possible arrangements of the order in which the six patients are taken are possible?   23.____

   A. 1   B. 2   C. 3   D. 4   E. 5 or more

24. Mrs. Cavity must be the _____ patient to be taken.   24.____

   A. 2nd   B. 3rd   C. 4th   D. 5th   E. 6th

25. If Miss Root's appointment is not last, what is the EARLIEST time she can be taken?   25.____

   A. 1:00 PM   B. 2:00 PM   C. 3:00 PM
   D. 4:00 PM   E. None of these

KEY (CORRECT ANSWERS)

1. B		11. B		
2. E		12. A		
3. C		13. C		
4. B		14. A		
5. C		15. D		
6. E		16. C		
7. B		17. E		
8. D		18. A		
9. E		19. E		
10. C		20. B		

21. D
22. B
23. D
24. D
25. E

SOLUTIONS TO PROBLEMS

For Questions 1-5, let the speeds corresponding to each auto be represented by the first letter of that auto. Then, since F = speed of a Ford, we can determine P = F - 15; C=F+20; D = $\frac{1}{2}$ F and D = P - 10; T > F. Thus, $\frac{1}{2}$ F = P - 10 and P = F - 15, which yields P = 35 m.p.h. and F = 50 m.p.h. Furthermore, C = 70 m.p.h., D = 25 m.p.h., and T > 50 m.p.h. Also, we know that T < 70 m.p.h.

1. Self-explanatory from the values obtained above.

(Answer B)

2. Self-explanatory.

(Answer E)

3. Since F = 50 m.p.h. and C = 70 m.p.h., therefore T = 60 m.p.h. (to be halfway between the speeds of a Ford and a Chevy). But, D.= 25, so that a Toyota is 35 m.p.h. faster than a Datsun.

(Answer C)

4. By doubling P, we get 70 m.p.h., it would exceed the speed of a Toyota, Ford, and Datsun.

(Answer B)

5. In symbols, B < 3P and B 4D. Thus 100 m.p.h. $\leq$ B < 105 m.p.h. Since the Buick's speed ends in a 0 or 5, its speed must be 100 m.p.h.

(Answer C)

For Questions 6-10 use the following matrix to show the availability of the nurse, doctor, and Vice Principal. Also, depict the times of Physical Education (P.E.) class.

	Before School	1st Period	Lunch	Last Period	After School
Monday	Nurse	P.E.			
Tuesday	Doctor			P.E.	Vice Principal
Wednesday	Nurse	P.E.			Doctor
Thursday				P.E.	Vice Principal, Doctor
Friday		P.E.			Vice Principal

6. The earliest time he (Jimmy) can get a doctor's note is Tuesday before school. Note that Jimmy could not get any written note from the nurse on Monday before school due to restriction 2. But by restriction 4, the Vice Principal cannot give a permission of excusal on Tuesday afternoon. After the nurse writes out a note on Wednesday before school, the next time the Vice Principal is available (Thursday after school), Jimmy can finally get an approval from the Vice Principal. Thus, by Friday 1st period, he can be excused from Physical Education class.

N.B. Recognize that the order in which any student will receive the approval notes is: Doctor, Nurse, Vice Principal.

(Answer E)

7.   By Tuesday, last period, Jimmy would have secured both the Doctor's note and the Nurse's note.

(Answer B)

8.   By the following Tuesday before school, Bobby will have the two required notes before the Vice Principal can issue an excuse note. The Vice Principal can issue this note on Tuesday after school and thus Bobby can get excused from the 1st period P.E. class on Wednesday.

(Answer D)

9.   Evident from the matrix.

(Answer E)

10.   The student could see the Doctor on Tuesday before school, the Vice Principal on Tuesday after school, and the Nurse on Wednesday before school. Thus, he would miss P.E. on Wednesday 1st period.

(Answer C)

For Questions 11-15, the following diagram is useful:

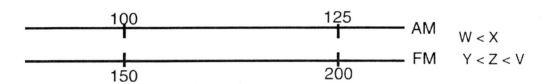

Notice that since the call number for Z is greater than that of X and the call number for Y is less than that of X, Z's number is greater than Y's.

11.   The equation FM = (2)(AM) - 50, will convert any AM station number to an FM station number and vice versa. Thus, if the call number is 110 AM, then the FM = (2)(110) - 50 = 170.

(Answer B)

12.   From all information given, the order must be WYXZV.

(Answer A)

13.   Since X > Y, and Y = 120, then X > 120.

(Answer C)

14.   In the equation FM = 2(AM) - 50, since Z = 180, the corresponding number on the AM dial is 115. Now, V > Z, so the corresponding AM number is > 115.

(Answer A)

15. Using the basic equation: $FM = 2(AM) - 50$, we know $P = 2W - 50$ where P, W are the call numbers of their respective stations. Also, $P = 2Z$. Thus, $2Z = 2W - 50$ and so $W = Z + 25$.

(Answer D)

QUESTIONS 16-19.

By using the first letters of the names of each speaker, Restriction 1 implies that the order of speaking was V, R, S. Restriction 2 implies that the order for all speakers was V, R, T, S, from first to last. Letting R = # of Robert's tips, T = # of Ted's tips, V = # of Vic's tips, and S = # of Sam's tips, you can deduce the following from restrictions 3, 4, and 5: $R < 2T$, $R = 1/3V$, $T = R - 5$, $S = \frac{1}{4}R$. Also, since Ted did not give the fewest number of tips, Sam gave the fewest number.

16. The reverse order of speakers must be S, T, R, V.

(Answer C)

17. Using $R < 2T$ and $T = R - 5$, we get $R < 2(R - 5)$, which gives $R > 10$. However, $S = \frac{1}{4}R$, so that the smallest R value allowable is 12. (If R were 11, $S = \frac{1}{4}(11) \neq$ a whole number).

(Answer E)

18. Since $R \geq 12$ and $R = 1/3V$, $V \geq 36$. Thus, 33 is not allowed.

(Answer A)

19. We know that $T + 5 = 1/3V$. Now $1/3V$ must be a whole number and if $V < 50$, V could be no higher than 48. This implies that $T + 5 \leq 1/3(48) = 16$. Now, $T \leq 11$. None of the choices given is correct.

(Answer E)

QUESTIONS 20-25.

Using a time line, four possibilities exist:

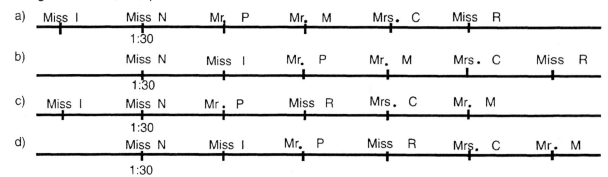

20. Since Mr. Pain's appointment is after 1:00 PM, the earliest it could be is 2:00 PM. Now condition 5 implies that Miss Injection's appointment could be no earlier than 1:00 PM. In this way Miss Injection's appointment is $\frac{1}{2}$ hour away from Miss Novocaine's, and 1 hour away from Mr. Pain's.

(Answer B)

21. Evident from the above time lines.

(Answer D)

22. If Mr. Pain's appointment is 2:30 PM or later, Miss Injection's appointment could be earlier than 1:00 PM (using possibility a) or c) above).

(Answer B)

23. Evident from the above time lines.

(Answer D)

24. Evident from the above time lines.

(Answer D)

25. Using time line c) above, Mr. Pain's appointment could be as early as 2:00 PM. Thus Miss Root's appointment could be as early as 2:30 PM. None of the given answers corresponds to this time.

(Answer E)

EXAMINATION SECTION
TEST 1

DIRECTIONS: Each question or incomplete statement is followed by several suggested answers or completions. Select the one that BEST answers the question or completes the statement. *PRINT THE LETTER OF THE CORRECT ANSWER IN THE SPACE AT THE RIGHT.*

QUESTIONS 1-7.

Questions 1-7 refer to the following information:

Seven individuals attended a picnic at Majestic View Park. No two of these people are the same age. The following information is also known:
    I.   Jack's age is exactly one-third of Ken's age and Jack is younger than Paula.
    II.   Oliver is 8 years older than Paula.
    III.   Laura's age plus Nancy's age equals Jack's age, but this sum is less than Mary's age.
    IV.   Ken's age is exactly double that of Paula's.
    V.   None of the seven individuals is younger than 10 years old nor older than 100 years old.
    VI.   Laura is not the youngest person.
    VII.   Mary's age is the average of Paula's age and Ken's age.

1. The OLDEST person is   1.____

    A. Laura   B. Mary   C. Ken
    D. Nancy   E. none of these

2. The LOWEST age that Jack could be is   2.____

    A. 12   B. 15   C. 18
    D. 21   E. 24

3. The HIGHEST age that Oliver could be is   3.____

    A. 58   B. 62   C. 66
    D. 70   E. 74

4. The individual who is *older* than 3 people and also *younger* than 3 people is   4.____

    A. Laura   B. Mary   C. Oliver
    D. Jack   E. none of these

5. How many individuals are *older* than Mary?   5.____

    A. 0   B. 1   C. 2
    D. 3   E. 4

6. If Jack were 30 years old, then Paula could be   6.____

    A. 33   B. 34
    C. 35   D. any of the above
    E. none of the above

7. Which of the following *correctly* lists the individuals by age in *ascending* order?　　　　7.___

    A. Laura, Nancy, Paula, Oliver, Jack, Mary, Ken
    B. Nancy, Jack, Paula, Laura, Oliver, Ken, Mary
    C. Laura, Jack, Nancy, Paula, Ken, Mary, Oliver
    D. Paula, Laura, Jack, Mary, Oliver, Ken, Nancy
    E. Nancy, Laura, Jack, Paula, Oliver, Mary, Ken

QUESTIONS 8-14.

Questions 8-14 refer to the following information.

Rose, Sue, Ted, Viola, and William went bowling at the Roll-E-Z Bowling Alley, where they each bowled one game. Although none of the bowlers revealed his/her score, the following is known:
    I.   No two bowlers had the same bowling score.
    II. A female bowled the lowest score, and she bowled last.
    III. Ted did NOT bowl the highest score, and he bowled third in the order.
    IV. William bowled before Ted, and he (William) bowled a better score than two bowlers.
    V. Viola's bowling score was better than Ted's score, and she bowled after Sue but before Rose.
    VI. Sue bowled after William.
    VII. In conditions V and VI, the expressions "bowled after" and "bowled before" do NOT necessarily mean "bowled directly after" or "bowled directly before."

8. The *second* bowler in the order was　　　　8.___

    A. Viola　　　　　　　　　　　B. Sue
    C. either Sue or William　　　　D. William
    E. Viola, Sue, or William

9. Rose bowled _____ in the order and scored _____.　　　　9.___

    A. first; second best　　　　　B. next to Last; second lowest
    C. last; lowest　　　　　　　　D. last; second lowest
    E. first; best

10. The CORRECT listing of bowlers from *first* to *last* is　　　　10.___

    A. Sue, William, Ted, Rose, Viola
    B. William, Viola, Ted, Rose, Sue
    C. Rose, William, Ted, Viola, Sue
    D. William, Sue, Ted, Viola, Rose
    E. Sue, Viola, Ted, Rose, William

11. Who bowled the highest score?　　　　11.___

    A. William or Sue　　　　　　B. Sue or Viola
    C. William or Viola　　　　　　D. Rose or Viola
    E. Rose or William

12. Ted's score was better than that of _____ other bowler(s).　　　　12.___

    A. 1　　　　　　　B. 3　　　　　　　C. 4
    D. either 3 or 4　　E. either 1 or 3

13. If Sue bowled better than Ted, which one(s) of the following is (are) necessarily TRUE?　13.____
    I.   Sue bowled worse than Viola.
    II. Ted bowled worse than William.
    III. Viola bowled the best.

    A. I *only*　　　　　　　　　B. II *only*
    C. III *only*　　　　　　　　D. *Exactly two* of the above
    E. All of the above

14. How many individuals bowled *after* William but *before* Sue?　14.____

    A. 0　　　　　　B. 1　　　　　　C. 2
    D. 0 or 1　　　E. 1 or 2

QUESTIONS 15-25.

Questions 15-25 refer to the following information:

Amy, Bob, Carl, Donna, Ellen, and Florence are six individuals whose professions are: artist, bookkeeper, counselor, doctor, engineer, and fashion designer, though not necessarily in that order. They earn six different annual salaries, each one of which is a multiple of $5000. Also:
    I.   The fashion designer is a female, but earns neither the lowest nor the highest salary.
    II.   Carl and the engineer are bowling partners with the doctor, the latter of whom earns the highest salary. None of the other individuals bowl.
    III. The artist earned two degrees from State University, which she attended during the same time that Amy was attending that school. Currently the artist earns more than two of the other five people, including Donna.
    IV.   Donna earns the least. Her steady boyfriend is the counselor, although she used to date the doctor.
    V.   The fashion designer and the engineer were Ellen's guests at the latter's wedding reception recently.
    VI.   The fashion designer earns more than the artist but less than the engineer.
    VII. Only the doctor earns more than Florence.
    VIII. The second highest income is $80,000 per year.
    IX.   If the annual incomes were arranged in ascending order, the largest difference between any two consecutive salaries is $15,000.
    X.   The fourth highest income is exactly double the lowest salary.
    XI.   Each person's annual salary exceeds $25,000.
    XII. The second lowest income is exactly one-third of the highest income.

15. The artist is　15.____

    A. Amy　　　　B. Bob　　　　C. Carl
    D. Donna　　　E. Ellen

16. _____ earned the HIGHEST salary and _____ earned the SECOND TO LOWEST salary.　16.____

    A. Bob; Carl　　　B. Amy; Donna　　　C. Ellen; Florence
    D. Bob; Ellen　　　E. Amy; Florence

17. Amy's annual salary is

   A. $60,000   B. $65,000
   C. between $65,000 and $80,000   D. between $60,000 and $80,000
   E. between $60,000 and $75,000

17.____

18. The doctor's MINIMUM salary is

   A. $80,000   B. $85,000   C. $90,000
   D. $95,000   E. none of these

18.____

19. _____ earns $40,000.

   A. Bob   B. Carl   C. Ellen
   D. Donna   E. none of these

19.____

20. The dollar difference between the counselor's and the artist's salary is

   A. $10,000   B. $15,000   C. $20,000
   D. $25,000   E. none of these

20.____

21. The individual whose salary CANNOT be determined exactly is the

   A. bookkeeper   B. doctor   C. fashion designer
   D. engineer   E. artist

21.____

22. Donna is the

   A. artist   B. bookkeeper   C. counselor
   D. engineer   E. none of these

22.____

23. The engineer earns more than _____ individual(s).

   A. 0   B. 1   C. 2
   D. 3   E. 4

23.____

24. The individuals who do NOT bowl are

   A. Donna, Bob, Florence   B. Donna, Bob, Ellen
   C. Donna, Amy, Ellen   D. Amy, Bob, Florence
   E. Amy, Florence, Donna

24.____

25. The CORRECT listing of the six individuals arranged from LOWEST salary to HIGHEST salary is

   A. Ellen, Amy, Carl, Donna, Bob, Florence
   B. Donna, Carl, Ellen, Amy, Florence, Bob
   C. Amy, Ellen, Florence, Carl, Donna, Bob
   D. Donna, Florence, Carl, Bob, Ellen, Amy
   E. Ellen, Donna, Carl, Amy, Bob, Florence

25.____

KEY (CORRECT ANSWERS)

1.	C		11.	B
2.	D		12.	E
3.	A		13.	B
4.	E		14.	A
5.	B		15.	E
6.	E		16.	A
7.	E		17.	D
8.	B		18.	B
9.	C		19.	E
10.	D		20.	D

21.	C
22.	B
23.	E
24.	C
25.	B

SOLUTIONS

For questions 1-7, let the ages corresponding to each person be represented by the first letter of the person's name($\underline{O}$ for Oliver, for example). The seven conditions given yield the following equations: $J = 1/3K$, $J < P$, $O = P + 8$, $J < M$, $L + N = J$, $L + N < M$, $K = 2P$, $10 \leq$ each person ≤ 100, $M = (P + K)/2$.

We recognize that Ken must be older than Jack and Paula. Also, since Jack is older than both Laura and Nancy, Ken is also older than Laura and Nancy. From the last equation, $M = (P + K)/2$, we know that Mary's age is between Paula's age and Ken's age; thus Ken is also older than Mary. Suppose Ken were younger than Oliver (i.e.: $K < O$). Since $K = 2P$ and $\underline{O} = P + 8$, we would get $2P < P + 8$ r $P < 8$. This, however is not possible, since each person is at least 10 years old.

1. Self-explanatory from the above paragraph.
   (ANSWER C).

2. We determine that since $L + N = J$, Jack is older than both Laura and Nancy, but further analysis reveals that he is younger than the other four people. It is given that Laura is not the youngest; thus Nancy must be. Now, the lowest age for anyone is 10, and since no two people have the same age, if Nancy were 10, then the lowest age for Laura would be 11. Thus Jack would be 21.
   (ANSWER D).

3. If Ken (who is the oldest) were 100 years old, Paula would be 50. By condition II, Oliver would be 58.
   (ANSWER A).

4. We already know that $P < M < K$, from the statements $M = (P + K)/2$ and Ken is the oldest. We want to know if Oliver is younger than Mary. (By condition II, we know that Oliver is older than Paula.) If $\underline{O} < M$, consider the fact that M is the average of P and K of P and 2P, which is 3P/2. This implies that $\underline{O} < 3P/2$. But $\underline{O} = P + 8$. Thus $P + 8 < 3P/2$, implying that $P > 16$, which is certainly true. Had $\underline{O} > M$, then $P < 16$, which is impossible since Paula is older than Jack and J 2:21. Thus Paula is the individual younger than 3 people.
   (ANSWER E).

5. Only Ken is older than Mary.
   (ANSWER B).

6. If $J = 30$, $K = 90$, then $P = \dfrac{1}{2} K = 45$.
   (ANSWER E).

7. Evident from information given in above explanations.
   (ANSWER E).

For 8-14 the following three matrices are possible. First letters of names are used.

Matrix 1

Bowling Order	1	2	3	4	last
Score					
Lowest					R
2			T		
3	W				
4		S			
Highest				V	

Matrix 2

Bowling Order	1	2	3	4	last
Score					R
Lowest					
2		S			
3	W				
4			T		
Highest				V	

Matrix 3

Bowling Order	1	2	3	4	last
Score					
Lowest					R
2			T		
3	W				
4				V	
Highest		S			

8. Only Sue could bowl second.
   (ANSWER B).

9. Rose will bowl last and score lowest.
   (ANSWER C).

10. Evident by reading the names from left to right in any of the three matrices.
    (ANSWER D).

11. Sue has the highest score in matrix 3; Viola is highest in matrices 1 and 2.
    (ANSWER B).

12. For matrix 1 or 3 Ted's score beat Rose's score, but in matrix 2, Ted scored second highest.
    (ANSWER E).

13. If Sue bowled better than Ted, then matrix 1 or 3 applies, and William bowled better than Ted. Matrix 3 does not support statements I and III.
    (ANSWER B).

14. If matrix 1 applies, the answer is 0. The answer is also 0 if matrix 2 or 3 applies.
    (ANSWER A).

For 15-25, the following matrix applies.

Salary Profession	Lowest	5th	4th	3rd	2nd	Highest
Artist			Ellen			
Bookkeeper	Donna					
Counselor		Carl				
Doctor						Bob
Engineer					Florence	
Fashion Designer				Amy		

15. Evident from the above matrix.
(ANSWER E).

16. Evident from the above matrix.
(ANSWER A).

17. Amy's salary is the 3rd highest and the 2nd highest is $80,000 by condition VIII. Now condition IX assures us that Amy's salary can be no lower than $65,000.
(ANSWER D).

18. In the opening introductory paragraph lor problems 15-25, we find that all salaries are multiples of $5000. Coupled with condition VIII, the minimum salary higher than 80,000 is 85,000.
(ANSWER B).

19. By using conditions VII through XII, we can determine the following: Lowest salary = $30,000; 5th highest = $35,000; 4th highest = $60,000; 3rd highest = $65,000 or $70,000 or $75,000; 2nd highest = $80,000; highest = $105,000. Thus, no one earns $40,000.
(ANSWER E).

20. The difference is $60,000 - $35,000 = $25,000.
(ANSWER D).

21. The 3rd highest salary cannot be determined exactly, and this corresponds to the fashion designer.
(ANSWER C).

22. Evident from the matrix.
(ANSWER B).

23. Evident from the matrix.
(ANSWER E).

24. From condition II, only Carl, the engineer (Florence), and the doctor (Bob) bowl.
(ANSWER C).

25. Evident from the matrix.
(ANSWER B).

EXAMINATION SECTION
TEST 1

DIRECTIONS: Each question or incomplete statement is followed by several suggested answers or completions. Select the one that BEST answers the question or completes the statement. *PRINT THE LETTER OF THE CORRECT ANSWER IN THE SPACE AT THE RIGHT.*

QUESTIONS 1-5.

Questions 1-5 refer to the following factual conditions.

Mrs. Jones is a teacher with a class of only five students, whose names are Alice, Bob, Carol, Donald, and Edna. There is only one row consisting of six seats, numbered 1 through 6 from front to back. No girl will sit behind all the other children. Also, due to conflicting personalities, Alice and Carol must not be assigned to consecutive seats.

1. Which of the following arrangements is(are) acceptable for seats #3 through #6?
    I.   Empty, Alice, Carol, Bob
    II. Carol, Donald, Edna, Empty
    III. Carol, Edna, Empty, Bob
The CORRECT answer is:

   A. I only   B. II only   C. III only
   D. I and II   E. II and III

2. If Alice is assigned to the fourth seat, and the two boys are assigned to the first and second seats, in how many ways can the remaining two girls be seated?

   A. 1   B. 2
   C. 3   D. 4
   E. None of these

3. If Edna, Donald, and Carol will be seated in consecutive seats (from front to back), in that order, in how many ways can all the students be arranged?

   A. 2   B. 3   C. 4   D. 5   E. 6 or more

4. If Mrs. Jones decides that the sixth seat shall be vacant and that Alice needs to sit in either the first or second seat, which of the following statements must be TRUE?

   A. The first seat will be occupied by a girl
   B. If Alice sits in the second seat, Edna will sit in either the first or third seats
   C. If Alice sits in the first seat, Carol will sit in the third seat
   D. The two boys will occupy the fourth and fifth seats
   E. None of the above

5. Suppose Edna is assigned the fifth seat and Donald is assigned the third seat. Which of the following represents the complete and accurate list of seat numbers which may be vacant?

   A. 2 and 4   B. 1 *only*   C. 4 and 6
   D. 1 and 2   E. 2 *only*

1.____
2.____
3.____
4.____
5.____

QUESTIONS 6-10.

Questions 6-10 refer to the following factual conditions.

John wishes to arrange seven textbooks on a shelf, which contains exactly seven slots numbered 1 through 7 from left to right. Three texts are math books, two are history books, one is a science book, and one is a logic book. He has decided that no two math books will occupy adjacent slots and that the number of slots between the two history books must equal the number of slots between the logic and science books. This number may be zero.

6. Which of the following arrangements for the first three slots is (are) NOT acceptable?   6.___
       I.   History, History, Math
       II.   History, Logic, History
       III.   Science, Math, Logic
    The CORRECT answer is:

    A. I only   B. II only   C. III only
    D. I and II   E. I and III

7. If the slots numbered 2, 6, and 7 are occupied by the texts history, science, and logic   7.___
    respectively, which of the following statements is CORRECT?

    A. A math book must be in slot 1
    B. The other history book must be in slot 3
    C. Both statements A and B
    D. Any arrangement of the remaining books is acceptable
    E. There is no possible arrangement that satisfies these conditions

8. If no math book is placed in slots 5 or 7, then: 8.___

    A. A math book is placed in slot 1
    B. The two history books must be in slot 3
    C. Both statement A and B
    D. Any arrangement of the remaing books is acceptable
    E. There is no possible arrangement that satisfies these condition

9. If the third, fourth, and fifth slots are occupied by a logic book, math book, and history   9.___
    book respectively, then in which of the following pairs of slots would it NOT be possible to
    place the other two math books?

    A. 2 and 6   B. 2 and 7
    C. 1 and 7   D. 1 and 6
    E. More than one choice among A, B, C, D

10. If two of the math books occupy slots 1 and 4 and a history book occupies slot 6, then   10.___
    which of the following is a complete list of types of books which may occupy slot 5?

    A. History   B. Logic
    C. Science   D. Two of the above
    E. All of the above

QUESTIONS 11-15.

Questions 11-15 refer to the following factual conditions.

A family consists of 6 members: Mother, Father, 2 sons, Frank and George, and 2 daughters, Helen and Ida. The dining room table is circular with six seats numbered 1 through 6. Seat 1 is located at the 12 o'clock position and the seats are numbered consecutively clockwise, and are evenly spaced. (e.g., seat 4 is at 6 o'clock).
The family has some peculiar rules when they sit at this table, i.e.:
1.   None of the sons will sit in seat 4;
2.   Mother and Father must be three seats apart;
3.   Helen will not sit next to Ida; and
4.   Frank insists on sitting next to Mother.

11.   If Father sits in seat 2 and Ida sits in seat 4, which of the following is a complete list of the people who can occupy seat 3?   11.____

    A.   George and Helen   B.   Frank *only*
    C.   George *only*   D.   Frank and George
    E.   Mother *only*

12.   If Frank sits in an even-numbered seat, which of the following is (are) TRUE?   12.____
      I.   Father sits in an even-numbered seat
      II.   George sits next to Father
      III. Ida sits next to George or Frank
      IV. Mother sits in an odd-numbered seat
The CORRECT answer is:

    A.   I, II   B.   II, IV   C.   I, III
    D.   II, III, IV   E.   I, III, IV

13.   Which of the following is an IMPOSSIBLE arrangement of the occupants of seats 1 through 3 respectively?   13.____

    A.   George, Helen, Father   B.   Frank, Ida, Father
    C.   Mother, Helen, George   D.   Ida, George, Mother
    E.   None of these

14.   If one of the daughters is assigned to seat 6, and Mother is assigned to seat 4, which of the following choices lists ALL the seats which could be occupied by Helen?   14.____

    A.   1, 3, 5   B.   2, 3, 6   C.   2, 6
    D.   1, 2, 3   E.   1, 3, 6

15.   If George and Father decide to sit next to each other, and Father sits in seat 5, which of the following selections MOST accurately describes who may sit next to George (besides Father)?   15.____

    A.   Helen or Frank   B.   Only Frank
    C.   Ida or Helen   D.   Ida, Helen, or Frank
    E.   Only Ida

QUESTIONS 16-20.

Questions 16-20 refer to the following factual conditions.

A company is moving to a new building and is going to rearrange the location of each of its departments. The list of departments are: Marketing, Personnel, Engineering, Research, Advertising, and Sales. The new building will contain eight floors, and each of the six departments will occupy a complete floor, (numbered 1 through 8 from bottom to top). The company president has issued several restrictions:

1. No department shall be situated such that there is a vacant floor both one floor below it and one floor above it simultaneously.
2. If a department is located on the 8th floor, it is permissible to have a vacancy on the 7th floor, but not on both the 6th and 7th floors simultaneously.
3. The 1st floor shall never be vacant
4. The Personnel department shall be located no higher than the 3rd floor.
5. The Sales department must be situated on either the 4th floor or the 5th floor.

16. Suppose the Marketing department is assigned to the 8th floor, and the Advertising department is assigned to the 2nd floor. Which of the following statements is ACCURATE?   16.____

    A. If the Engineering department is on a higher floor than Personnel, then the Engineering department cannot be on the 3rd floor
    B. The Research department will necessarily be on a higher floor than Personnel
    C. If the 6th floor is occupied by Research, then the 7th floor must be occupied by Engineering
    D. If personnel is assigned to the 3rd floor, some department will be assigned to the 5th floor or there will be 2 consecutive vacancies
    E. If the 4th floor is vacant, then exactly two departments are situated on higher floors than Sales

17. Which of the following is a possible arrangement for the 1st floor through the 4th floor respectively?   17.____
        I.   Marketing, Vacant, Personnel, Sales
        II. Personnel, Vacant, Engineering, Vacant
        III. Research, Personnel, Sales, Marketing
    The CORRECT answer is:

    A. I only   B. II only   C. III only
    D. II, III   E. I, II, III

18. Which of the following is a possible arrangement for floors 5 through 8, respectively?   18.____
        I.   Vacant, Sales, Advertising, Engineering
        II. Vacant, Reaserch, Engineering, Vacant
        III. Sales, Marketing, Research, Advertising
        IV. Sales, Vacant, Vacant, Research
    The CORRECT answer is:

    A. I, II, III, IV
    B. Exactly one of I, II, III, IV
    C. Exactly two of I, II, III, IV
    D. Exactly three of I, II, III, IV
    E. None of the above

19. Suppose that Marketing is assigned to the 7th floor, and Advertising is assigned to the 3rd floor. After each of the other departments are then assigned to their respective floors, which of the following is a pair of floors for which vacancies can exist *simultaneously?*   19.____

    A. 1, 2   B. 4, 5   C. 2, 4   D. 6, 8   E. 5, 6

20. Assume that the Research department must be on a higher floor than Engineering but on a lower floor than Sales, and Personnel is below each of the other 5 departments. If Research occupies a floor no higher than the 5th, which of the following is a complete and accurate list of the floors on which it is possible to find Research?   20.____

    A. 2   B. 3 or 4   C. 3, 4, or 5
    D. 3   E. 4 or 5

QUESTIONS 21-25.

Questions 21-25 refer to the following factual conditions.

    A music teacher needs to select four students to play in a small band. The selected students will sit in seats 1 through 4, from left to right. The instruments being played from seat 1 to seat 4 IN ORDER are: trumpet, trombone, saxophone, and drum. Students A and B can only play trumpet. Student C can play trumpet or saxophone. Student D can play trombone or drum. Student E can only play trombone. Students G and H can only play saxophone. Students J and K can only play drums. (Assume that any one person cannot be chosen to play 2 instruments simultaneously.) Additionally, 2 other stipulations prevail:
    1. D will not participate if J is chosen to play.
    2. B will participate only if H is also chosen.

21. Which of the following is a possible selection for seats 1 to 4, respectively?   21.____
        I. A, D, H, J
      II. B, E, H, D
     III. C, D, H, K
The CORRECT answer is:

    A. I *only*   B. II *only*
    C. III *only*   D. Exactly 2 choices of I, II, III
    E. I, II, III

22. If B is chosen to play trumpet, in how many different ways can the other three players be chosen?   22.____

    A. 3   B. 4   C. 5   D. 6   E. 7

23. Which of the following statements would be sufficient to imply that A will play trumpet?   23.____

    A. C is chosen for saxophone
    B. E is chosen for trombone, and G is chosen for saxophone
    C. D is chosen for trombone
    D. All of the above
    E. None of the above

24. If H is chosen for saxophone, and K is chosen for drum, this implies 24.___

    A. C is chosen for trumpet
    B. B is chosen for trumpet
    C. E is chosen for trombone
    D. Exactly 2 of A, B, or C must be correct
    E. None of A, B, C must necessarily be correct

25. Which of the following statements is ACCURATE? 25.___

    A. If A plays trumpet, then C plays saxophone
    B. If D plays trombone, then K play drum
    C. If G plays saxophone, then C plays trumpet
    D. If K plays drum, then E plays trombone
    E. None of the above

———

KEY (CORRECT ANSWERS)

1. C		11. C	
2. E		12. E	
3. D		13. D	
4. B		14. B	
5. D		15. C	
6. D		16. D	
7. E		17. A	
8. A		18. C	
9. E		19. E	
10. E		20. B	

21. D
22. B
23. A
24. E
25. B

———

SOLUTIONS TO PROBLEMS

1. CHOICE I is not acceptable since Alice and Carol sit in consecutive seats.
   CHOICE II is not acceptable since Edna would be sitting behind everyone else, violating the condition that no girl shall sit behind all the other children.
   CHOICE III is acceptable, for it allows the following complete seating arrangement: Alice, Donald, Carol, Edna, Empty, Bob.

   (Answer C)

2. Regardless of how Carol and Edna are seated, one girl will be sitting behind all the other children, which is not a per-missable condition.

   (Answer E)

3. The allowable arrangements are:
   Alice, Empty, Edna, Donald, Carol, Bob
   Empty, Alice, Edna, Donald, Carol, Bob
   Edna, Donald, Carol, Empty, Alice, Bob
   Alice, Edna, Donald, Carol, Empty, Bob
   Alice, Edna, Donald, Carol, Bob, Empty

   (Answer D)

4. CHOICE A is not necessarily true, since Alice could be assigned to the second seat, and either Donald or Bob could be assigned the first seat.
   CHOICE B must take place; since, if Edna sat in the fourth seat, Carol would be forced into either the first, second, or fifth seats. This would violate one of the required conditions that either Alice and Carol cannot occupy consecutive seats, or that no girl shall sit behind all the other children.
   CHOICE C need not happen, since a possible arrangement is: Alice, Bob, Edna, Carol, Donald, Empty.
   CHOICE D is not necessarily true, as seen in the explanation of CHOICE C.

   (Answer B)

5. Bob must be assigned to the sixth seat, in order not to violate the required conditions. If seat 4 were vacant, it would force Alice and Carol to sit in consecutive seats. If the first seat were vacant, Alice and Carol could occupy seats 2 and 4. Likewise, if the second seat were vacant, Alice and Carol could occupy seats 1 and 4. Thus, CHOICE D is correct and complete.

   (Answer D)

6. CHOICE I would force the other two math books into slots 5 and 7 and thus the logic and science books would be 2 slots apart. Since the history books are not 2 slots apart also, this is incorrect.
   CHOICE II implies that the science book would occupy slot 4 and this situation would force the math books to occupy adjacent slots.
   CHOICE III is acceptable, with the following complete arrangement: Science, Math, Logic, Math, History, Math, History.

   (Answer D)

7. From the stated conditions in the paragraph governing this question, a history book must be placed in either slot 1 or slot 3. In either event, as least one pair of adjacent slots (numbers 4 and 5) will both contain math books.

(Answer E)

8. CHOICE A implies that the other two math books will be found in slots 1 and 6. Since the number of slots between the two history books must equal the number of slots between the number of slots between the science and logic books, the history books can be placed in slots 2 and 4, with the science and logic books in slots 5 and 7.
CHOICE B is not necessarily true since a possible arrangement is: Logic, Math, History, Math, Science, Math, History.
CHOICE C would place the math books in slots 1, 4, and 6. Thus the science and logic books could not be adjacent to each other.
CHOICE D would create a five-slot gap requirement for the two history books, which is impossible.
CHOICE E can be countered by this arrangement: Math, History, Math, History, Logic, Math, Science.

(Answer A)

9. CHOICES B and D would be impossible. For CHOICE B, we have _____, Math, Logic, Math, History, _____, Math. No matter how the other history and science books are filled in, a violation of the original conditions will prevail. For CHOICE D, we would have Math, _____ Logic, Math, History, Math, _____. Again no possible arrangement of the remaining two books is permissible.

(Answer E)

10. CHOICE A allows this arrangement: Math, Logic, Science, Math, History, History, Math. Also the logic and science books may be interchanged.
CHOICE B allows: Math, Science, History, Math, Logic, History, Math.
CHOICE C allows: Math, Logic, History, Math, Science, History, Math.
Thus all 3 of the subjects history, logic, and science are allowed.

(Answer E)

11. Condition 3 eliminates Helen from seat 3. Frank cannot occupy seat 3 either because of condition 4. If Mother were to occupy seat 3, then Frank would be forced into seat 5 or seat 6, — again violating condition 4. George could be assigned seat 3 and an acceptable arrangement becomes: Helen, Father, George, Ida, Mother, Frank.

(Answer C)

12. Due to condition 1, Frank must sit in seat 2 or seat 6. By condition 4, Mother will definitely sit in an odd-numbered seat. By condition 2, this implies that Father will sit three seats away from Mother and this will be an even-numbered seat. Statement II is not necessarily true as the following arrangement shows: Mother, Frank, Helen, Father, Ida, George. Thus, statements I, III, and IV must be true.

(Answer E)

13. CHOICE D will violate one of the four conditions. By condition 4, Frank would be forced into seat 4. However, this situation would violate condition 1. Each of choices a, b, c are possible, as indicated with the following complete arrangements associated with each of these choices.
For CHOICE A: George, Helen, Father, Ida, Frank, Mother
For CHOICE B: Frank, Ida, Father, Helen, George, Mother
For CHOICE C: Mother, Helen, George, Father, Ida, Frank

(Answer D)

14. Certainly Helen could occupy seat 6, from the given information. If Ida is assigned seat 6, then Helen cannot occupy seats 1 or 5. Since Mother is already in seat 4, Helen is then obliged to take seats 2 or 3. Thus, seats 2, 3, or 6 are the only ones which Helen may occupy.

(Answer B)

15. Condition 4 forces Frank to sit in seat 1 or seat 3, which follows from condition 2 placing Mother in seat 2. The only arrangements which would then allow Frank to sit next to George would be as follows (seats 1 to 6 in order):
    1. Frank, Mother, _____, _____, Father, George; or
    2. _____, Mother, Frank, George, Father, _____
Actually arrangement (2) is NOT allowed due to condition 1, and neither of these arrangements are permitted by condition 3. This, logic leads one to eliminate Frank as an eligible candidate to sit next to George. Either Ida or Helen (CHOICE C) may sit next to George since the final arrangement can be:
    Ida, Mother, Frank, Helen, Father, George; or
    Helen, Mother, Frank, Ida, Father, George

(Answer C)

16. For the purposes of abbreviation, the letters A, E, M, P, R, and S will be used to refer to each department. V means vacancy.
CHOICE A is not accurate since one possible arrangement could be: P, A, E, S, V, V, R, M (other arrangments also exist).
CHOICE B can be shown incorrect by this arrangement: R, A, P, V, S, E, V, M. The arrangement E, A, P, V, S, R, V, M shows
CHOICE C to be false.
CHOICE D is correct. Suppose Sales is not assigned to the 5th floor. Then the first 4 floors would be E or R, A, P, S. Now, if no department is assigned to the 5th floor, then the 2 vacant floors would be the 5th and 6th or the 5th and 7th. But having the vacancies on the 5th and 7th floors would violate restriction 1. Thus, vacancies on the 5th and 6th floors represent 2 consecutive vacancies.
CHOICE E places the Sales department on the 5th floor. But we could have vacancies on the 3rd and 4th floors so that the final arrangement is: P, A, V, V, S, E, R, M. Thus 3 departments are located on higher floors than Sales.

(Answer D)

17. CHOICE I violates no restriction, and can be completed for floors 5 through 8 as:
    Research, Engineering, Advertising, Vacant.
CHOICE II violates restriction 1.
CHOICE III violates restriction 5.

(Answer A)

18. CHOICE I violates restriction 5.
    CHOICE II is acceptable and the 1st through 4th floors could be occupied by Marketing, Advertising, Personnel, Sales.
    CHOICE III is also acceptable and here the first 4 floors could be Engineering, Personnel, Vacant, Vacant.
    CHOICE IV is not correct due to restriction 2.

(Answer C)

19. The pair 1, 2 is eliminated because of restrictions 3 and 4.
    The pair 4, 5 is eliminated because of restriction 5.
    The pair 2, 4 would create a violation of restriction 1.
    The pair 6, 8 also violates restriction 1.
    However, the pair 5, 6 can be both vacant. The completed arrangement must have Personnel on the 1st or 2nd floors and Sales on the 4th floor.

(Answer E)

20. Since Sales must be located on either the 4th or 5th floor, Research cannot be located on floor 5, and thus we have narrowed the selection to floors 1, 2, 3, or 4. But Personnel must occupy floor 1, since it is below all other departments (Recall, the 1st floor cannot be vacant). Also, Research must be higher than Engineering, so floor 2 cannot be occupied by Research. Either floors 3 or 4 are possible as shown by the following schemes: P, E, R, S, V, V, A, M or P, E, V, R, S, A, M, V (for example).

(Answer B)

21. Stipulation 1 eliminates selection I. Selections II and III are both permissible. Recognize that stipulation 2 does not preclude H from being chosen when B is not chosen.

(Answer D)

22. For seats 2, 3, 4, the four possibilities are: (1) D, H, K; (2) E, H, D; (3) E, H, J; and (4) E, H, K. Note that H MUST be selected due to stipulation 2.

(Answer B)

23. Once C is chosen for saxophone, only A or B are left as eligibles for trumpet. Now H has been eliminated, and thus stipulation 2 precludes B from playing. Thus CHOICE A is correct.
    In CHOICE B, the final selection could be C, E, G, _____, where any of D, J, or K may play drum. Thus A need not be chosen.
    In CHOICE C, selections exist for which A, B, or C will play trumpet.

(Answer A)

24. The final selection could be A, D, H, K and so none of the statements A, B, C need necessarily be correct.

(Answer E)

25. In CHOICE A, combinations exist where either G or H may play saxophone. Examples
        are: A, D, G, K and A, E, H, K.
     In CHOICE B, once D is selected for trombone, only J and K remain eligible for drum.
        However, stipulation 1 forces K to be selected.
     In CHOICE C, we could have A, D, G, K.
     In CHOICE D, again, the selection of A, D, G, K is possible.
     Thus, only CHOICE B is accurate.

  (Answer B)

———————

EXAMINATION SECTION
TEST 1

DIRECTIONS: Each question or incomplete statement is followed by several suggested answers or completions. Select the one that BEST answers the question or completes the statement. *PRINT THE LETTER OF THE CORRECT ANSWER IN THE SPACE AT THE RIGHT.*

QUESTIONS 1-5.

Questions 1-5 refer to the following factual conditions.

A person has five animals to care for. They are a dog, cat, alligator, horse, and rabbit. These animals will be kept in an area with 5 joining compartments, numbered 1 through 5 from left to right. Only 1 animal is allowed per compartment. Two other conditions must be met:
1. The dog and cat must not be kept in adjacent compartments unless the horse is kept in a compartment adjoining either one of them, since the horse's temperament is a stabilizing factor.
2. The horse is the only animal which is not afraid of the alligator. Thus, no other animal may be placed next to the alligator.

1. Which of the following is NOT possible concerning the arrangement of the animals in the last 3 compartments?   1.____
    I.   dog, horse, alligator
    II. dog, horse, cat
    III. cat, dog, rabbit
The CORRECT answer is:

    A. I *only*
    B. II *only*
    C. III *only*
    D. Exactly two choices of I, II, III
    E. All three choices of I, II, III

2. If the alligator is placed in compartment 4, which arrangement is MOST proper?   2.____

    A. The cat is placed in compartment 1
    B. The horse is placed in compartment 5
    C. The rabbit is placed in any compartment except 2
    D. No arrangement is possible
    E. The horse is placed in either compartments 3 or 5

3. Which of the following is a complete and accurate list of the compartment(s) which may be occupied by the rabbit?   3.____

    A. Any compartment   B. 1, 2, and 3
    C. 5 *only*   D. 2 and 4 *only*
    E. Any compartment but 3

4. If the horse is placed in compartment 2, in how many ways can the dog and cat be placed in the other compartments?   4.____

    A. 2   B. 3   C. 4   D. 5   E. 6

5. If the cat is not placed in compartment 3, which of the following is a complete list of animals which could occupy compartment 3?   5.____

    A. horse, dog   B. rabbit   C. alligator, dog
    D. rabbit, dog   E. dog

QUESTIONS 6-11.

Questions 6-11 refer to the following factual conditions.

Six people are standing in a line at a movie theater, one behind the other. The individuals are numbered 1 through 6 from front to back. The theater is showing three movies entitled W, X, and Y. It is known that each of the six people has a ticket for exactly one of these movies. Also, the following conditions are known:
1. The 4th person has a ticket for either X or Y.
2. There is one individual standing between the two people who have tickets for X.
3. For the 3 people who have a ticket for W, exactly 2 of them are standing one behind the other. The third person with a ticket for W is standing neither directly in front of nor directly behind either of the other two.

6. Which of the following is an acceptable arrangement of the movie selections corresponding to the first 4 people?   6.____

    A. XWXY   B. WWWX   C. WXWY   D. XWWX   E. XYXW

7. Which of the following is(are) acceptable as position numbers for the individuals holding a ticket for X?   7.____

    I. 2, 4
    II. 4, 6
    III. 1, 3
The CORRECT answer is:

    A. I *only*
    B. II *only*
    C. III *only*
    D. Exactly 2 choices of I, II, III
    E. All three choices of I, II, III

8. Which of the following is the most complete and accurate group of numbered positions of people who can hold a ticket for Y?   8.____

    A. 4   B. 2, 4   C. 1, 4   D. 1, 3, 4   E. 1, 2, 4

9. If the third person in line has a ticket for W, then which of the following must be true?   9.____

    A. The 4th person holds a ticket for Y
    B. The 4th person holds a ticket for X
    C. The 5th and 6th persons both hold the other 2 tickets for W

D. The 2nd person holds a ticket for X
E. The 1st person holds a ticket for W

10. Assuming that the 1st person does NOT have a ticket for W, then the 2nd person will have a ticket for   10.____

    A. W *only*   B. X *only*   C. Y *only*
    D. Either W or X   E. Either X or Y

11. If the 5th and 6th individuals have tickets for X and W respectively, in how many ways can the other people be arranged?   11.____

    A. 1   B. 2   C. 3   D. 4   E. at least 5

QUESTIONS 12-18.

Questions 12-18 refer to the following factual conditions.

The Racing Secretary of Hoofbeats Raceway is about to assign eight horses their respective post positions (numbered 1 through 8) in today's feature race. The horses' names are: Applesauce, Bologna, Celery, Derma, Edible, Fruit Cup, Green Bean, and Honey Pie. The following restrictions apply:
1. Neither Applesauce nor Celery may be assigned to Post 1 or Post 8.
2. Derma must race from an even numbered post.
3. Bologna and Fruit Cup must both be assigned odd numbered posts.
4. Green Bean's post number must be smaller than that of Honey Pie.
5. Edible's post number must be higher than that of Honey Pie, but smaller than that of Fruit Cup.

12. Which of the following is a complete and accurate list of who may race from Post 1?   12.____

    A. Bologna, Fruit Cup, Honey Pie
    B. All but Applesauce and Celery
    C. Bologna, Green Bean
    D. only Green Bean
    E. Bologna, Derma, Fruit Cup, Green Bean

13. To what post numbers may Green Bean be assigned?   13.____

    A. 1, 2   B. 1, 2, 3   C. 2, 3, 4
    D. 1, 2, 3, 4   E. 1, 2, 3, 4, 5

14. If Applesauce is assigned to post 3 and Celery is assigned to post 4, which of the following horses cannot be assigned to post 5?   14.____

    A. Green Bean   B. Bologna   C. Fruit Cup
    D. Honey Pie   E. Edible

15. How many different horses would be eligible to be assigned to post 8?   15.____

    A. 1   B. 2   C. 3   D. 4   E. 5 or 6

16. All of the following are acceptable arrangements of the horses assigned to posts 2, 3, and 4 respectively EXCEPT: 16.____

    A. Applesauce, Bologna, Celery
    B. Honey Pie, Fruit Cup, Edible
    C. Celery, Green Bean, Honey Pie
    D. Green Bean, Honey Pie, Edible
    E. Honey Pie, Applesauce, Edible

17. Which of the following gives the complete list of horses which CANNOT race from post 7?   17.____

    A. Derma, Edible, Fruit Cup, Green Bean
    B. Celery, Derma, Edible, Green Bean
    C. Derma, Edible, Green Bean, Honey Pie
    D. Derma, Edible, Fruit Cup, Green Bean, Honey Pie
    E. Bologna, Celery

18. Which restriction(s) could be removed WITHOUT affecting the solutions to the preceding questions?   18.____

    A. 1 and 3   B. 2 and 5   C. 1   D. 2   E. 5

QUESTIONS 19-22.

Questions 19-22 refer to the following factual conditions.

The work assignments are rather peculiar for the five employees of the Frozen prices Supermarket. Following are the work conditions:
1. Jack can only work on Mondays and Saturdays.
2. Lisa can work any days except Saturdays and Sundays.
3. Melanie can work on any days, provided at least one of the other four employees is also working on those days.
4. Nancy will only work on days when no one else is assigned.
5. Otto can work any days except Wednesdays. Also, since he cannot tolerate Lisa, he will not work on any day that she is assigned.

19. The MAXIMUM number of workers who can be assigned Tuesdays is   19.____

    A. 1   B. 2   C. 3   D. 4   E. 5

20. If the manager decides to assign 3 workers for Saturday, which of the following group(s) could be assigned?   20.____

    A. Jack, Melanie, Otto
    B. Nancy, Otto, Jack
    C. Jack, Lisa, Melanie
    D. Exactly two selections of A, B, and C
    E. None of the above

21. During one particular week (Sunday through Saturday), the manager decides to have Lisa work on only 2 days, which must be consecutive. Otto will be unable to work on Saturday, but he will also only work on 2 consecutive days. Nancy is assigned to work only on Monday.
On which 2 consecutive days can Lisa work?

21.____

    A. Monday, Tuesday
    B. Tuesday, Wednesday
    C. Thursday, Friday
    D. Friday, Saturday
    E. Sunday, Monday

22. Refer to the situation in the previous question. If Jack is assigned to work only 1 day, what is the MAXIMUM number of days on which Melanie can work (during that week)?

22.____

    A. 3   B. 4   C. 5   D. 6   E. 7

QUESTIONS 23-25.

Questions 23-25 refer to the following factual conditions.

A child is about to color in 4 pages of a coloring book, using only one color on each page. The available colors are yellow, red, and green; but not every color is required to be used. Certain conditions will also apply:
1. The number of pages colored in green cannot exceed the number of pages colored in red.
2. The 3rd page must be colored in yellow or red.
3. No two consecutive pages will have the same color.

23. If page 2 is colored red, which one(s) of the following arrangements is(are) possible for pages 1 through 4, respectively?

23.____

    A. Yellow, red, yellow, green
    B. Yellow, red, yellow, red
    C. Yellow, red, green, red
    D. Exactly 2 selections of A, B, and C
    E. All of the above

24. If page 1 is colored green, how many different coloring arrangements are possible for the other pages?

24.____

    A. 0   B. 1   C. 2   D. 3   E. 4

25. For which of the following conditions is it possible that NO page will be colored green?

25.____

    A. Page 1 is red
    B. Pages 1 and 3 are different colors
    C. Pages 1 and 4 are both yellow
    D. All selections of A, B, C
    E. None of A, B, C

KEY (CORRECT ANSWERS)

1.	B		11.	B
2.	D		12.	C
3.	E		13.	D
4.	C		14.	A
5.	E		15.	A
6.	A		16.	B
7.	E		17.	C
8.	D		18.	D
9.	B		19.	B
10.	D		20.	A

21.	B
22.	C
23.	D
24.	C
25.	A

———

SOLUTIONS TO PROBLEMS

1. CHOICE I can be allowed no matter how the cat and rabbit are arranged.
   CHOICE II is impossible, since whether the alligator is placed in the first or second compartments, condition 2 will be violated.
   CHOICE III is allowed provided that the first compartment is occupied by the alligator and the second one by the horse.

   (Answer B)

   1.____

2. Once the alligator is placed into compartment 4, two other animals must occupy adjacent compartments. This situation violates condition 2.

   (Answer D)

   2.____

3. If the horse is placed in compartment 4 with the alligator in compartment 5, then the rabbit can be put in either compartments 1 or 2. Similarly, by placing the alligator and horse in compartments 1 and 2 respectively, the rabbit can be put in compartments 4 or 5. Recognizing that the alligator must be put in compartments 1 or 5, if the rabbit were placed in compartment 3, we would have alligator, _____, rabbit, _____, _____ or _____, _____, rabbit, _____, alligator. In either situation, the horse must be placed between the rabbit and alligator. But then condition 1 will be violated.

   (Answer E)

   3.____

4. Following are the only allowable arrangements:
   1. alligator, horse, cat, rabbit, dog
   2. alligator, horse, cat, dog, rabbit
   3. alligator, horse, dog, rabbit, cat
   4. alligator, horse, dog, cat, rabbit

   (Answer C)

   4.____

5. It is already known that the alligator must be in compartments 1 or 5 and that the rabbit cannot be in compartment 3. Thus, only the horse and dog are left as candidates. But in order not to violate condition 2, the horse will have to be placed in compartment 2 or 4. Thus, only the dog can occupy compartment 3.

   (Answer E)

   5.____

6. We know that 1 person has a ticket for Y, 2 have tickets for X, and 3 have tickets for W.
   CHOICE A would read as: XWXYWW, and thus all conditions are satisfied.
   CHOICE B violates condition 3.
   CHOICE C also violates condition 3.
   CHOICE D violates condition 2.
   CHOICE E violates condition 1.

   (Answer A)

   6.____

7. CHOICES I, II, III can be shown as respectively WXYXWW, YWWXWX, and XWXYWW.

   (Answer E)

   7.____

8. The solutions given above for problem #7 show Y in positions 1, 3, and 4. If Y were placed in position 2, this would force X into position 4 (by condition 1). However, by condition 2, we would then have to place X also in position 6. The three remaining slots would be filled by W's but would violate condition 3. A similar contradiction would occur if Y were in position 5. (Note that position 6 WOULD be a legal place for Y.)   8.___

(Answer D)

9. If the 4th person had a ticket for Y, then condition 2 could not be satisfied no matter which two people have tickets for X. By condition 1, the 4th person must have a ticket for X. The arrangement of YWWXWX shows that choices C, D, and E need not be true.   9.___

(Answer B)

10. If the 1st person has a ticket for X, then so must the 3rd person also have a ticket for X. This implies that the 4th person has a ticket for Y (by condition 1) and that the remaining people (including the 2nd person) have tickets for W. However, if the 1st person has a ticket for Y, then the 4th person has a ticket for X. At this point, the 2nd individual could also have a ticket for X, so that the 3rd, 5th, and 6th persons have tickets for W.   10.___

(Answer D)

11. We know that of the other 4 people, 2 have tickets for W, 1 has a ticket for X, and 1 has a ticket for Y. In order to satisfy all three initial conditions of the problem (given in the paragraph preceding question 6), the arrangement of tickets must be WWXYXW. But the 2 people who have tickets for W (besides the 6th person) can be interchanged.   11.___

(Answer B)

12. Restrictions 1 and 2 eliminate Applesauce, Celery, and Derma from post 1. Restriction 4 implies that Honey Pie must race from a post 2 or higher. Restriction 5 implies that both Edible and Fruit Cup must have post numbers higher than 2. Thus, only Bologna and Green Bean are candilates for post 1.   12.___

(Answer C)

13. From restrictions 4 and 5, Green Bean, Honey Pie, Edible, and Fruit Cup must have post numbers in ascending order. This would normally imply that Green Bean's post number could be as high as 5. But, by restriction 3, Fruit Cup cannot have a post number higher than 7. Thus, Green Bean's highest post number could only be 4.   13.___

(Answer D)

14. The explanation to question #13 provides the rationale for Green Bean not possibly being assigned to post 5. The only other horse not allowed post 5 would be Derma (restriction 2).   14.___

(Answer A)

15. Restriction 3 eliminates Bologna and Fruit Cup from post 8. Restriction 5 implies that the post numbers assigned to both Edible and Honey Pie must be less than Fruit Cup's. Thus, neither of them is eligible for post 8. Question #13 removes Green Bean from consideration, while restriction 1 eliminates both Applesauce and Celery. Only Derma may race from post 8.   15.___

(Answer A)

16. CHOICE B violates restriction 5, CHOICES A, C, D, and E could be satisfied with the following corresponding complete arrangements (using the first letters of the first name to abbreviate):
    For CHOICE A: GABCHEFD
    For CHOICE C: BCGHEAFD
    For CHOICE D: BGHEFACD
    For CHOICE E: GHAEBCFD

    (Answer B)

16.____

17. Restriction 2 could have been deleted, since we discovered from question #15 that Derma must race from post 8.

    (Answer C)

17.____

18. The highest post number for Fruit Cup is 7. By restriction 5, Edible's and Honey pie's post numbers must be less than that of Fruit Cup. Derma must be assigned post 8. Restriction 4 implies that Green Bean's post number must also be less than 7.

    (Answer D)

18.____

19. Both Lisa and Melanie could be assigned. Restriction 1 eliminates Jack, restriction 4 precludes Nancy, and by restriction 5, Otto will not work when Lisa is assigned. Note that both Melanie and Otto could be assigned, too.

    (Answer B)

19.____

20. CHOICE A violates no restrictions.
    CHOICE B is eliminated by restriction 4.
    CHOICE C is eliminated by restriction 2.
    Since only one choice among A, B, and C is correct, CHOICES D and E must be incorrect.

    (Answer A)

20.____

21. CHOICES D and E are not applicable due to restriction 2. Since Nancy is assigned to work on Monday, restriction 4 would prohibit Lisa from also working on Monday. Thus, CHOICE A is eliminated. By deduction, the only 2 consecutive days for Otto to work are Thursday and Friday. Thus Lisa must work Tuesday and Wednesday, due to restriction 5.

    (Answer B)

21.____

22. Since Nancy is already working on Monday, the only day left for Jack to work is Saturday. By restriction 3, Melanie will not be able to work on Sunday, and restriction 4 prevents her from working on Monday. Thus, she can work for 5 days maximum.

    (Answer C)

22.____

23. The arrangements for CHOICES A and B are acceptable. However, CHOICE C violated restriction 2. Thus, CHOICE D is correct.

    (Answer D)

23.____

24. For pages 2 through 4, the only acceptable arrangements are red, yellow, red and yellow, 24.___
red, yellow.

(Answer C)

25. If page 1 is red, the sequence of all 4 pages could be red, yellow, red, yellow. If pages 1 25.___
and 3 were different, the third color would have to be used on page 2 (restriction
3). Finally, if pages 1 and 4 were both yellow, page 3 must be red. This would result in
the same situation as described above in the second sentence.

(Answer A)

———————

ANSWER SHEET

TEST NO. _____ PART _____ TITLE OF POSITION _____

(AS GIVEN IN EXAMINATION ANNOUNCEMENT - INCLUDE OPTION, IF ANY)

PLACE OF EXAMINATION _____ DATE_____

(CITY OR TOWN)   (STATE)

RATING

USE THE SPECIAL PENCIL. MAKE GLOSSY BLACK MARKS.

	A B C D E		A B C D E		A B C D E		A B C D E		A B C D E
1	:: :: :: :: ::	26	:: :: :: :: ::	51	:: :: :: :: ::	76	:: :: :: :: ::	101	:: :: :: :: ::
2	:: :: :: :: ::	27	:: :: :: :: ::	52	:: :: :: :: ::	77	:: :: :: :: ::	102	:: :: :: :: ::
3	:: :: :: :: ::	28	:: :: :: :: ::	53	:: :: :: :: ::	78	:: :: :: :: ::	103	:: :: :: :: ::
4	:: :: :: :: ::	29	:: :: :: :: ::	54	:: :: :: :: ::	79	:: :: :: :: ::	104	:: :: :: :: ::
5	:: :: :: :: ::	30	:: :: :: :: ::	55	:: :: :: :: ::	80	:: :: :: :: ::	105	:: :: :: :: ::
6	:: :: :: :: ::	31	:: :: :: :: ::	56	:: :: :: :: ::	81	:: :: :: :: ::	106	:: :: :: :: ::
7	:: :: :: :: ::	32	:: :: :: :: ::	57	:: :: :: :: ::	82	:: :: :: :: ::	107	:: :: :: :: ::
8	:: :: :: :: ::	33	:: :: :: :: ::	58	:: :: :: :: ::	83	:: :: :: :: ::	108	:: :: :: :: ::
9	:: :: :: :: ::	34	:: :: :: :: ::	59	:: :: :: :: ::	84	:: :: :: :: ::	109	:: :: :: :: ::
10	:: :: :: :: ::	35	:: :: :: :: ::	60	:: :: :: :: ::	85	:: :: :: :: ::	110	:: :: :: :: ::

Make only ONE mark for each answer. Additional and stray marks may be
counted as mistakes. In making corrections, erase errors COMPLETELY.

	A B C D E		A B C D E		A B C D E		A B C D E		A B C D E
11	:: :: :: :: ::	36	:: :: :: :: ::	61	:: :: :: :: ::	86	:: :: :: :: ::	111	:: :: :: :: ::
12	:: :: :: :: ::	37	:: :: :: :: ::	62	:: :: :: :: ::	87	:: :: :: :: ::	112	:: :: :: :: ::
13	:: :: :: :: ::	38	:: :: :: :: ::	63	:: :: :: :: ::	88	:: :: :: :: ::	113	:: :: :: :: ::
14	:: :: :: :: ::	39	:: :: :: :: ::	64	:: :: :: :: ::	89	:: :: :: :: ::	114	:: :: :: :: ::
15	:: :: :: :: ::	40	:: :: :: :: ::	65	:: :: :: :: ::	90	:: :: :: :: ::	115	:: :: :: :: ::
16	:: :: :: :: ::	41	:: :: :: :: ::	66	:: :: :: :: ::	91	:: :: :: :: ::	116	:: :: :: :: ::
17	:: :: :: :: ::	42	:: :: :: :: ::	67	:: :: :: :: ::	92	:: :: :: :: ::	117	:: :: :: :: ::
18	:: :: :: :: ::	43	:: :: :: :: ::	68	:: :: :: :: ::	93	:: :: :: :: ::	118	:: :: :: :: ::
19	:: :: :: :: ::	44	:: :: :: :: ::	69	:: :: :: :: ::	94	:: :: :: :: ::	119	:: :: :: :: ::
20	:: :: :: :: ::	45	:: :: :: :: ::	70	:: :: :: :: ::	95	:: :: :: :: ::	120	:: :: :: :: ::
21	:: :: :: :: ::	46	:: :: :: :: ::	71	:: :: :: :: ::	96	:: :: :: :: ::	121	:: :: :: :: ::
22	:: :: :: :: ::	47	:: :: :: :: ::	72	:: :: :: :: ::	97	:: :: :: :: ::	122	:: :: :: :: ::
23	:: :: :: :: ::	48	:: :: :: :: ::	73	:: :: :: :: ::	98	:: :: :: :: ::	123	:: :: :: :: ::
24	:: :: :: :: ::	49	:: :: :: :: ::	74	:: :: :: :: ::	99	:: :: :: :: ::	124	:: :: :: :: ::
25	:: :: :: :: ::	50	:: :: :: :: ::	75	:: :: :: :: ::	100	:: :: :: :: ::	125	:: :: :: :: ::

ANSWER SHEET

TEST NO. ________ PART ______ TITLE OF POSITION ____
(AS GIVEN IN EXAMINATION ANNOUNCEMENT - INCLUDE OPTION, IF ANY)

PLACE OF EXAMINATION ______________________________ ______________________ DATE ________
(CITY OR TOWN) (STATE)

RATING

USE THE SPECIAL PENCIL. MAKE GLOSSY BLACK MARKS.

1 A B C D E	26 A B C D E	51 A B C D E	76 A B C D E	101 A B C D E
2 A B C D E	27 A B C D E	52 A B C D E	77 A B C D E	102 A B C D E
3 A B C D E	28 A B C D E	53 A B C D E	78 A B C D E	103 A B C D E
4 A B C D E	29 A B C D E	54 A B C D E	79 A B C D E	104 A B C D E
5 A B C D E	30 A B C D E	55 A B C D E	80 A B C D E	105 A B C D E
6 A B C D E	31 A B C D E	56 A B C D E	81 A B C D E	106 A B C D E
7 A B C D E	32 A B C D E	57 A B C D E	82 A B C D E	107 A B C D E
8 A B C D E	33 A B C D E	58 A B C D E	83 A B C D E	108 A B C D E
9 A B C D E	34 A B C D E	59 A B C D E	84 A B C D E	109 A B C D E
10 A B C D E	35 A B C D E	60 A B C D E	85 A B C D E	110 A B C D E

Make only ONE mark for each answer. Additional and stray marks may be counted as mistakes. In making corrections, erase errors COMPLETELY.

11 A B C D E	36 A B C D E	61 A B C D E	86 A B C D E	111 A B C D E
12 A B C D E	37 A B C D E	62 A B C D E	87 A B C D E	112 A B C D E
13 A B C D E	38 A B C D E	63 A B C D E	88 A B C D E	113 A B C D E
14 A B C D E	39 A B C D E	64 A B C D E	89 A B C D E	114 A B C D E
15 A B C D E	40 A B C D E	65 A B C D E	90 A B C D E	115 A B C D E
16 A B C D E	41 A B C D E	66 A B C D E	91 A B C D E	116 A B C D E
17 A B C D E	42 A B C D E	67 A B C D E	92 A B C D E	117 A B C D E
18 A B C D E	43 A B C D E	68 A B C D E	93 A B C D E	118 A B C D E
19 A B C D E	44 A B C D E	69 A B C D E	94 A B C D E	119 A B C D E
20 A B C D E	45 A B C D E	70 A B C D E	95 A B C D E	120 A B C D E
21 A B C D E	46 A B C D E	71 A B C D E	96 A B C D E	121 A B C D E
22 A B C D E	47 A B C D E	72 A B C D E	97 A B C D E	122 A B C D E
23 A B C D E	48 A B C D E	73 A B C D E	98 A B C D E	123 A B C D E
24 A B C D E	49 A B C D E	74 A B C D E	99 A B C D E	124 A B C D E
25 A B C D E	50 A B C D E	75 A B C D E	100 A B C D E	125 A B C D E